FEMpower

Transformational Stories of Women
Thriving Against All Odds

Inspired by the Authors' Speeches at the
United Nations

Compiled by Visionary Author,

Dr. Elayna Fernández

FEMpower
Transformational Stories of Women Thriving Against All Odds

Compiled by Dr. Elayna Fernández

Copyright© 2024 and beyond by Elayna Fernández ~ the Positive MOM

All rights reserved. No part of this book may be reproduced or transmitted in any form or by any means without written permission from the authors.

The scanning, uploading, and distribution of this book without the author's permission is theft of the authors' intellectual property. The purchaser of this book may scan or copy it for personal use only. You may post a quote on social media platforms only if accompanied by author credit and the hashtag #transformationalstorytellers.

Disclaimer: The authors do not guarantee that anyone following these recommendations or suggestions will gain any specific results. The information in this book does not and is not intended to constitute legal, psychological, or medical advice. The authors shall have neither liability nor responsibility to anyone concerning any loss or damage caused or alleged to be caused directly or indirectly by the information contained in this book.

The opinions expressed in these chapters are solely the authors' and do not reflect or represent the opinions or beliefs of the visionary author and/or publisher. Authors have assured that no content submitted to publisher infringes on any copyright, design, privacy, publicity, data protection, trademark, or any other rights of any third party, and is not obscene, abusive, threatening, libelous, or defamatory of any person.

Content Warning: The stories in this book include references to sexual violence, domestic violence, neglect and abuse, suicide and self-harming disorders, eating disorders, abortion, mental illness, bullying, poverty, discrimination, shame, addiction and substance misuse, sexual harassment, exploitation and assault, and other content types that may be upsetting, challenging, or triggering.

If you or someone you know is struggling with suicidal thoughts, call or text 988 or chat at 988lifeline.org.

For intimate partner violence support, call the National Domestic Violence Hotline at 1.800.799.SAFE (7233) or text "START" to 88788.

Developmental editing by Elayna Fernández
Published by thePositiveMOM.com

To all women and girls around the world.
We believe in your greatness and your divinity.

Table of Contents

Introduction: Against All Odds, by Dr. Elayna Fernández............. 1

Chapter 1: Create S.P.A.C.E.: Five Steps to Transform Workplaces for Women's Empowerment, by Carmen Paredes... 5

Chapter 2: How to Have Extraordinary Impact: One Table at a Time, by Dr. Zoe-Ann Hayden Bartlett 17

Chapter 3: Our Voices: Shape Optimal Healthcare Journeys Through Advocacy, by Lidia Molinara ... 29

Chapter 4: Suicide Prevention: How to Be a SAFE Person and S.A.V.E. Lives, by Dr. Elayna Fernández 39

Chapter 5: How to Find Strength For Every Struggle and Season In Motherhood, by Mirella Acebo 51

Chapter 6: How to Create Happiness Through the Social Influences of Mental Health, by Dr. Julie Radlauer 61

Chapter 7: Three Reasons to Celebrate Your Scars and Live the Best Version of Yourself, by Dr. Jiyoung Jung 71

Chapter 8: How to Transform Your Timid Team Members Into Confident Powerhouses, by Mary Ottman 81

Chapter 9: Five Strategies for Enhancing Reproductive Health and Personal Growth for Women, by Amb. Dr. Catherine Utsalo 93

Chapter 10: One Tool to End the Stigma of Hair Loss, by Stephanie L. Anderson 105

Chapter 11: How to Protect People with Disabilities from Partnership Abuse, by Shāna Boutté 117

Chapter 12: Three Steps to Your PATH to Thrive, by Britt Ivy Boice 127

Conclusion: Your Power to Thrive, by Dr. Elayna Fernández ..141

References 143

Against All Odds

by Dr. Elayna Fernández

On July 31, 2024, a select group of women presented speeches at the United Nations in support of empowering women and girls and promoting gender equality.

I was honored to be part of this initiative as both a speaker and a leader, guiding the speakers in crafting and delivering their talks, and more recently, in expanding each of their narratives into chapters of this book.

As you read their words, you will feel their passion and learn how they overcame seemingly insurmountable odds to become the inspiring women they are today.

In our individual and collective work, we are committed to contributing to the 17 Sustainable Development Goals (SDGs):

1. **No Poverty** – Ending poverty in all forms
2. **Zero Hunger** – Achieving food security and promoting sustainable agriculture
3. **Good Health and Well-being** – Ensuring healthy lives and promoting well-being for all ages

4. **Quality Education** – Inclusive, equitable education for all
5. **Gender Equality** – Achieving gender equality and empowering women and girls
6. **Clean Water and Sanitation** – Access to clean water and hygiene for everyone
7. **Affordable and Clean Energy** – Reliable and sustainable energy for all
8. **Decent Work and Economic Growth** – Promoting economic opportunities and fair work
9. **Industry, Innovation, and Infrastructure** – Building resilient infrastructure and innovation
10. **Reduced Inequalities** – Reducing inequality within and among countries
11. **Sustainable Cities and Communities** – Making cities safe, inclusive, and sustainable
12. **Responsible Consumption and Production** – Ensuring sustainable consumption and production
13. **Climate Action** – Taking urgent action to combat climate change
14. **Life Below Water** – Conserving oceans and marine life
15. **Life on Land** – Protecting ecosystems, forests, and biodiversity
16. **Peace, Justice, and Strong Institutions** – Promoting peace, justice, and inclusivity
17. **Partnerships for the Goals** – Strengthening global and local partnerships

I always say that "your adversity is not your destiny," and each S.T.O.R.Y. in this book demonstrates this truth. No matter where you are right now, what you're thinking, what you're feeling, or what resources you do or don't have, you have the possibility and the power to transcend your circumstances.

Our individual triumphs and efforts can solve the global challenges we face today. It's not only our duty, but our privilege to create a better world where we all can rise and thrive.

The women in this book have turned their goals into a game plan to empower others, and so can you. Let's start now!

Create S.P.A.C.E.: Five Steps to Transform Workplaces for Women's Empowerment

by Carmen Paredes

One percent!

When I realized that "for every 100 leadership roles, only one is occupied by a Latina," it shook me to my core.

I wasn't expecting that reading a McKinsey report on a Sunday morning would turn my weekend upside down, but the truth was that this data hit me hard, as it painted a stark and troubling picture, one that I've experienced myself.

Despite the progress we've made as a society, women, even though they make up more than half of today's workforce, only hold 35% of top leadership positions across industries. The disparity was glaring, almost mocking me, and with each statistic in the report, my sense of unease deepened.

But the figure that truly struck me the most—the one that left me feeling physically ill—was this: Latinas, women just like me, make up less than 1% of those top leadership positions.

This isn't just a statistic; it's a painful reality that reflects the deep-seated challenges and barriers that still exist for women in the corporate world.

The numbers weren't just disheartening; they were a painful reminder of the work that still needs to be done.

Perhaps this statistic hit me really hard because I've experienced this truth firsthand. For 20 years, I poured everything I had into my career, working myself to the brink of death after burning out. There were nights when I cried myself to sleep, overwhelmed by the pressure and the seemingly insurmountable obstacles that stood in my way.

As an immigrant, the so-called "American dream" was more than just an aspiration; it was a promise I had made to myself. But there were times when that dream felt so far out of reach that I almost gave up.

But one cold Alaskan afternoon when I was about to throw in the towel, something happened that changed everything. Against all odds, my hard work finally paid off.

I can still recall the moment with vivid clarity. At first, I was in such a state of shock that I couldn't find the words. My mind was a whirlwind of emotions, and for a brief moment, I thought I must be dreaming. So, I did what anyone in my position would do—I pinched myself. The sharp sting brought me back to reality. This was real.

This achievement wasn't just a personal victory; it was a milestone that carried with it a profound sense of responsibility. On that day, I became one of the few women to rise to the rank of Vice President in a male-dominated industry. But more importantly, I became the first Latina Vice President at the largest telecommunications company in Anchorage, and quite possibly, the first Latina Vice President in the entire state of Alaska. It felt as though I had been invited to sit at King Arthur's round table, a place where power, influence, and responsibility converged.

But with this new title came the understanding that my success was not just about me. It was about the countless women who would come after me, women who needed someone to pave the way, to open doors that had long been closed to them. It was this realization that led me to initiate a movement—a movement to create S.P.A.C.E.

S.P.A.C.E., in this context, is not about creating emptiness. Instead, it's about enriching our workplaces with positive change, opportunities for growth, and the essential support systems that allow women to thrive. For over two decades, I've been in the trenches—leading, mentoring, coaching, speaking, and facilitating workshops aimed at uplifting and empowering women to navigate the often treacherous waters of professional life.

This movement, which is encapsulated in the acronym S.P.A.C.E.— Standards, Protection, Awareness, Culture, and Expression— represents the foundational pillars that I believe are essential for empowering women of all backgrounds and ages and transforming workplaces into environments where everyone can succeed.

Let's explore each pillar in more detail:

1. Standards: The Bedrock of Empowerment

Standards are the bedrock of any organization. They define what is acceptable, what is expected, and what will not be tolerated.

In the context of women's empowerment, enforced standards are crucial for creating a safe and supportive work environment. When standards are clear and enforcement is consistent, we create a workplace where women can work without fear of harassment or discrimination.

Consider this: According to a study by Catalyst, workplaces that enforce high standards of conduct see a reduction in harassment and discrimination complaints by up to 50%. This isn't just about compliance; it's about fostering a culture of respect, where every employee feels valued and protected. Besides, when women feel safe at work, they are more likely to perform at their best, leading to increased productivity, higher morale, and reduced turnover rates.

But let's take this a step further. I invite you to reflect on your own workplace. Are the standards in your organization truly enforced? Do they protect women from discrimination and harassment? If not, what can you do to advocate for change?

It's not enough to have policies on paper; they must be actively implemented and upheld. This requires commitment from leadership and accountability at all levels of the organization. As leaders, it is our responsibility to ensure that our workplaces are not just compliant with the law, but also places where everyone can thrive.

2. Protection: Building Strong Support Systems

Protection comes in many forms. Protection is about creating a strong support system for women in the workplace, one that includes mentorship, advocacy, and the provision of resources necessary for their professional growth. In the journey of professional advancement, having someone to guide, mentor, and protect you can make all the difference.

According to McKinsey, establishing protective support systems, such as mentorship programs, can increase the representation of women in senior management roles by as much as 30%.

This is significant, as mentorship provides women with the guidance they need to navigate the complexities of corporate life, and it creates a sense of belonging and inclusion. When women know they have someone in their corner, they are more likely to take risks, pursue leadership opportunities, and remain committed to their career goals.

But mentorship is just one aspect of protection. It also includes advocating for women's rights in the workplace, ensuring that they have access to the same opportunities as their male counterparts, and providing the resources they need to succeed. This could mean anything from offering leadership development programs to creating flexible work arrangements that allow women to balance their professional and personal responsibilities.

So, let me ask you: Does your workplace have a mentorship program specifically designed for women? If it doesn't, do you have the influence or the opportunity to initiate one?

A mentorship program can be a powerful tool for empowering women, providing them with the guidance and support they need to navigate the often-challenging corporate landscape.

Beyond mentorship, consider what other forms of protection your organization offers. Are women given the same opportunities for advancement as men? Are there policies in place to ensure pay equity? Protection is about more than just safety; it's about creating an environment where women can thrive.

3. Awareness: Recognizing and Addressing Bias

Awareness is about recognizing the unique challenges that women face in the workplace and taking deliberate action to address them. This can be achieved through regular training sessions that cover topics such as diversity, inclusion, unconscious bias, and bystander intervention.

Fostering awareness in the workplace is not just about checking a box; it's about creating a culture where everyone is conscious of the biases that exist and is committed to addressing them.

Studies show that companies that prioritize diversity and inclusion training see up to a 70% increase in creativity and innovation. This is because diverse teams bring a wider range of perspectives to the table, leading to more creative solutions and better decision-making.

Awareness isn't just about attending a training session; it's about integrating this knowledge into everyday practices. It's about being mindful of the language we use, the assumptions we make, and how we interact with others. It's about creating an environment where everyone feels included and valued, regardless of their gender, race, or background.

So, think back to the past year: Have you participated in any diversity and inclusion training? If so, how have you applied what you learned in your daily interactions? If not, why not?

Awareness is a continuous process, and it requires ongoing effort to maintain. It's about being proactive in identifying and addressing the biases that exist in our workplaces and taking steps to create a more inclusive environment.

4. Culture: The Lifeblood of Organizations

Awareness naturally leads us to Culture. Culture is the lifeblood of any organization. It sets the behavioral norms and values that influence how employees interact with one another and with the company as a whole.

A positive, inclusive culture is one that accepts diversity and celebrates it. Such culture can enhance engagement and productivity by 27% on average. It attracts top talent and, most importantly, supports women's empowerment.

Creating a culture of inclusion requires more than just policies and procedures; it requires a commitment from leadership to model inclusive behavior. This means creating opportunities for everyone to contribute, recognizing and celebrating diversity, and fostering an environment where everyone feels they belong. It's about creating a workplace where differences are not just tolerated but embraced.

An inclusive culture isn't just the responsibility of leadership; it's something that every employee can contribute to. It's about being mindful of the way we interact with others, being open to different perspectives, and being willing to challenge the status quo. It's about creating an environment where everyone feels safe to bring their whole selves to work, knowing that they will be valued and respected.

Take a moment to reflect on your own workplace culture. Do you think your team members would say that you celebrate diversity? Is your workplace one where everyone, regardless of gender, feels included and valued? Building an inclusive culture takes time and intentionality, but the rewards are immense. When everyone feels like they belong, they are more engaged, more productive, and more likely to stay with the company.

5. Expression: Ensuring Women's Voices Are Heard

Expression is about ensuring that the voices of women are heard and considered at all levels of the organization.

When women feel comfortable voicing their concerns, ideas, and perspectives, decision-making processes improve significantly— by up to 20%, according to recent articles from the Harvard Business Review.

This isn't just about improving decisions; it's about fostering a sense of belonging and respect. Women need to know that their voices matter and that their contributions are valued. This means creating opportunities for women to speak up, whether it's in meetings, through formal feedback channels, or in one-on-one conversations with leadership.

Creating S.P.A.C.E. for expression isn't just about giving women a seat at the table; it's about ensuring that their voices are heard and respected. This means actively listening to what women have to say, taking their feedback seriously, and acting on it. It's about creating a culture where everyone feels safe to speak up, knowing that their contributions will be valued and respected.

Reflect on this: Do you believe that women in your workplace feel comfortable expressing their concerns and ideas? If not, what steps can you take to create an environment where they do?

Moving From Thought to Action: The Call to Empowerment

Because you are reading this book, I'm going to take a wild guess and assume that like me, you are deeply committed to empowering women. The ideas we've discussed today aren't just theoretical; they're practical steps that we can all take to create meaningful change in our workplaces. But to make a real impact, we need to move from thought to action.

The journey to empowerment isn't a sprint; it's a marathon. It requires dedication, perseverance, and a commitment to creating lasting change. By focusing on these five pillars—Standards, Protection, Awareness, Culture, and Expression—we can build workplaces that support women and celebrate their achievements. We can create environments where women feel safe, valued, and empowered to reach their full potential.

And this journey isn't one that we take alone. It's a collective effort, one that requires the participation of everyone in the organization, including you.

Your title does not matter. Whether you're a leader, a manager, or an employee, you have a role to play in creating a more inclusive, supportive workplace.

Maya Angelou once said, "Do the best you can until you know better. Then when you know better, do better."

Today, as we've explored the S.P.A.C.E. framework—Standards, Protection, Awareness, Culture, and Expression—you've gained new insights and new knowledge.

You know better. Now, you can use this knowledge to do better.

I invite you now to think of someone in your workplace—perhaps a colleague, a mentor, or even a member of senior management—with whom you can discuss the importance of creating S.P.A.C.E. for women.

Write down their name on a piece of paper and commit to having that conversation. It might be the first step in a larger movement within your organization.

Together, we can create workplaces where everyone feels valued, supported, and empowered to reach their full potential—including women.

Let's not just fill the spaces in our workplaces; let's fill them with purpose, with growth opportunities, and with the unwavering belief that everyone, regardless of gender, has a right to succeed.

I challenge you to take action, to be the change you want to see in your workplace, and to commit to creating S.P.A.C.E. for women to thrive.

Together, we can make a difference. Together, we can create S.P.A.C.E.

S.T.O.R.Y. Compiled by Dr. Elayna Fernández

2X TEDx speaker and Lifetime Presidential Award recipient Carmen Paredes is an award-winning keynote speaker and leadership transformation expert. With over 20 years of experience, she helps organizations grow profits and impact by teaching their leaders the principles of exceptional leadership. Learn more at ExceptionalLeadershipSolutions.com/keynote-speaker and follow @iamcarmenparedes.

How to Have Extraordinary Impact: One Table at a Time

by Dr. Zoe-Ann Hayden Bartlett

I sat at our family kitchen table for the last time. My chest felt hollow, like someone had taken a melon baller to my heart, scooping out pieces one memory at a time.

In our home, the table—once vibrant with laughter and conversation—now stood vacant and lonely, suspended in a state of complete stillness.

My childhood home was small, with our table positioned at its heart. It was the first thing anyone saw upon entering any room in the living space, and that honey-colored wooden table, shipped from Maine decades before by the military, stood like a beacon. Now, it was devoid of those who once gave it life.

When we sat around the table as a family, Mom sat closest to the kitchen, and I sat across from her, my back against the wall, observing everything. She made us laugh with her silly antics in the kitchen, like when she accidentally made "tuna" sandwiches out of cat food. And just like Dorothy from *The Wizard of Oz* clicking her red shoes and saying, "There's no place like home," home was our kitchen table.

As I continued to reflect, looking at the table on the bright, crisp winter day with expansive blue skies, typical of Eastern New Mexico, the house was eerily quiet. All I could hear were the distant wind chimes dancing in the breeze from the backyard. Perhaps they were the songs of angels welcoming my mom, Virginia, to a place without suffering. She had been laid to rest next to my Dad that morning, exactly 60 days after I'd turned 50. Mom had always been my best friend, mentor, and our family matriarch.

When I got the call late at night that Mom had passed, I was visiting Kauai on a much-needed holiday, just past the six-week recovery mark from a complete hysterectomy. I wished I could have been there with her, but my heart was content knowing I had helped her recover when she was in hospice.

Sitting at the table, I was grateful that she was a fighter—not many people "graduate" from hospice, but she did, which gave me a few more years with her.

She must have known she was about to make her transition. She called me that final morning, and her last words to me were: "Zoe, I love you...I really love you."

The memories flooded back like a river as I sat in my chair at the table at my parents' home that morning. For as long as I could recall, Mom would say, "Remember the stories that make you laugh when I'm gone." Just then, a grin crept across my face as I ran my hands over the tabletop, feeling the dimples and divots from years before, when she'd mistakenly sprayed oven cleaner on the table instead of furniture polish.

That memory and hundreds more were etched into the table's history, and it

became clear to me: if tables could talk, they would tell the stories of our lives.

Since then, tables have been on my mind. I chose to leave my award-winning corporate career working for Fortune 100 companies in global travel management to pursue heart-centered entrepreneurial work in the early 2000s. My transition wasn't just a career shift, but a profound personal metamorphosis driven by a desire to create meaningful work for myself and make a difference.

My journey began with consulting and was punctuated by a transformative experience abroad where I fulfilled a lifelong dream to attend culinary school. My French experience served to crystallize my vision, and the table stood squarely at the epicenter. I founded my company, Intentional Table, in 2010.

The first two years were spent orchestrating small events and writing about the unsung heroes who produce our food ethically. I then moved to a charming island off the coast of Seattle, and with the help of the landlord who shared my vision and had worked as a producer on major cooking shows, we transformed an old toy store and art gallery into a beautiful and vibrant food and wine studio.

This wasn't merely a business for me, but a living laboratory of human connection. The events, classes, and culinary tours became more than experiences—they were intentional gatherings that strengthened the community fabric, one table at a time. Though economic realities eventually led me to close the physical studio, the core mission remained undiminished. My sole focus for over a decade has been researching and collecting stories about how intentional tables unite, inspire, and positively impact lives and communities.

I'm eternally grateful for the reflective moments at my own family table that inspired my journey to this work. The research confirms that tables can serve to unite, equalize, and restore hope, and they can also be a force for good in dealing with the issues our society is facing. Now, more than ever, we need reasons to come together, instead of slipping further into segregation.

Today, humanitarian issues abound in every possible category and expose an uncomfortable reality—societal structure and our communities are in crisis. To recognize a few:

- Almost half of all countries worldwide are involved in active conflicts outside their borders, the highest since WWII.
- The political division has never been higher and is accelerated by partisan media.
- Global migration is outpacing population growth.
- Climate change is a significant threat to human health, the environment, and ecosystems.
- Widening income inequality is a crucial challenge of our time.
- The loneliness epidemic has been declared a global health threat.

We can all agree that these statistics and issues are heart-wrenching.

My own research and experiences reveal how tables can offer hope in our divided world. That's why I developed the T.A.B.L.E. framework. It demonstrates that tables provide a unique space where human stories can be shared and heard, weaving threads of compassion across cultural and social divides. The significance of this work has been recognized internationally, and I've had invitations to share these findings on the TEDx stage in Zimbabwe, Africa, and the United Nations. I believe that the table may be the only place big enough to hold our complex human story.

The gathering is a fleeting moment—seemingly ordinary yet potentially transformative. These moments hold the extraordinary power to reshape culture, cultivate courage, and forge deep connections. Through five diverse stories from my vast collection, you are about to read how one ordinary person can create extraordinary change, one table at a time.

T – Teaching moments that inspire action
A – Advocacy and community building
B – Breaking boundaries
L – Love, courage, and compassion
E – Educating ourselves and others

T. Teaching moments that inspire action

Dennis felt isolated after immigrating from Haiti to America as a young boy.

He stood out—not by choice, but by circumstance, due to a significant language barrier and a brand-new school. The result was social isolation.

A wise teacher saw his struggle and encouraged him to consider embracing his adversity, making it a teaching moment that inspired action.

With his teacher's support, Dennis devised an inclusive program so that no one would eat alone at his school. He didn't want his classmates to feel as excluded and lonely as he had, especially at the cafeteria table. This intentional program became a conduit for empathy. It rippled outwards and joined two other programs, all designed to empower students to create communities of belonging and eliminate social isolation in schools, where the loneliness epidemic is among the highest in society. That one small act has grown, and it now reaches over 10,000 schools and over 5 million students globally.

A. Advocacy and community building

Kristen's story began with an F in French class, which eventually set the stage for something remarkable. She went abroad to learn the French language and discovered the soul of French Culture.

In particular, she discovered long leisurely meals around the table, without devices, and with meaningful conversation. Years later, and now with her own young family, Kristen craved the connection she experienced during her time in France at the table. She wanted that for her own family and her community.

She painted a simple wooden picnic table a beautiful turquoise color, the universal color of hospitality, and placed it in the front yard, close to the street. Little by little, at the table, strangers became friends, and friends became the community she'd hoped for.

The intentional turquoise table invites neighbors to pause, connect, and belong. It's more than just furniture; it's a catalyst for change. Turquoise tables and the front yard movement have become symbols of unity and connection and are now found across the United States and several countries worldwide.

B. Breaking Boundaries

JR's story began in the concrete jungle of the projects, in the vibrant world of graffiti art. As he honed his skills and pushed the boundaries of creativity, JR wanted his work to extend beyond the confines of galleries and museums and be accessible to everyone.

He eventually developed an innovative large-scale photographic collage technique that became his signature calling. He wanted his art to spark meaningful conversation and touch the deepest part of our humanity, drawing attention to the forgotten and marginalized. One of his large-scale projects was a giant table on the border between the US and Mexico, a site of great contention for both countries.

Imagine a photograph of a young Mexican child's face. Now zoom in on this photo until only the pure and innocent eyes of this child are visible. This is the image that JR printed onto a vinyl tablecloth over 60 feet in length.

He stretched the tablecloth across the border of the two countries strategically, placing one of the photographed eyes on each side of the wall.

The table was enormous and impossible to miss. Soon, it attracted hundreds of Mexicans and Americans alike. Curious bystanders, hikers, and even the U.S. border patrol took a seat at this significant intentional table. They shared a meal while passing drinks and snacks to each other across the border.

The table served as a powerful reminder to the world that despite the walls and borders that divide us, we are all human beings. Walls and borders will not and cannot separate us.

L. Love, Courage, and Compassion

Jerilyn's story began long ago with the loss of her brother, a helicopter pilot who sacrificed his life during the Vietnam War.

Years later, reflecting on the loss of not only her brother but of so many people in Vietnam, she and her husband formed an organization dedicated to planting trees where there were once bombs and landmines in the region of Vietnam that was most scarred by the tragedy.

This important work has been going on for almost three decades and has expanded to helping to build schools, homes, and libraries, positively touching the lives of over 100,000 Vietnamese.

Perhaps one of the most poignant parts of this story, though, takes place as two former enemies meet across a table, face to face, decades after the horrific violence. Deep in each other's eyes, they see the horrors and the lasting effects of war. Each man shares their stories through the wisdom of their years.

The table allowed them to set down their differences and find forgiveness. In the quiet moments of their intentional table, each veteran found the true power of courage and compassion.

E. Educating ourselves and others

When Kelly learned about the staggering reality of human trafficking, she was profoundly moved and determined to make a difference. She invited close friends over for dinner and awkwardly asked them to contribute the equivalent cost of the meal.

Her two goals were to share what she had learned and to raise money for the cause.

That was over ten years ago. Today, Kelly and her husband continue to host these impactful dinners, hosting guests from near her community and guests from far away who come to participate.

Through their efforts, they've made significant donations and, just as importantly, raised awareness about this vile crime. Their gatherings have become a powerful force for freedom, educating others, and inspiring action in the fight against human trafficking.

In a world often fractured by division, there exists a simple yet profound instrument of unity: the table. More than just a piece of furniture, it is a sacred space where human stories converge, where differences dissolve, and where understanding takes root.

Each gathering around a table is an act of radical hope and extends the opportunity to bridge the chasms that separate us. These are not just gatherings; they are quiet revolutions of empathy and connection.

Imagine a table where strangers become friends, where political opponents focus on listening instead of arguing, and where cultural differences transform into a shared humanity. This is the power of an intentional table. Here, we don't just share food; we share our stories, our vulnerabilities, and our hopes.

Each person who sits at the table carries an extraordinary potential for change. An ordinary individual can create a ripple of understanding, compassion, and healing. These are not grand gestures, but intimate moments of human connection that slowly rebuild the fabric of our families, friends, and our communities.

The table becomes a neutral ground, a place where hierarchy dissolves, where titles and backgrounds fade, and where our shared human experience takes center stage. It is a democracy-filled space that whispers: "Here, we are equal. Here, we listen. Here, we connect."

In a society increasingly divided by screens and digital distances, the physical act of gathering around a table becomes a revolutionary statement. It says we choose presence over pixels, dialogue over discord, understanding over judgment.

This is more than an idea—it's a movement. A commitment to rebuilding social trust, one conversation at a time. By partnering with storytellers, community leaders, and individuals who believe in the transformative power of genuine connection, I am committed to help reimagine how we relate to one another.

The table doesn't just hold our meals, it holds our potential for mutual understanding.

It doesn't just support our plates, it supports our shared humanity. Each table is a silent witness—a keeper of moments both ordinary and extraordinary.

The Intentional Table project invites you to become a storyteller. By sharing your story, you're not just recording a memory—you're creating a living, breathing global heirloom that transcends individual lifetimes. Your narrative becomes part of a collective tapestry, connecting strangers through the universal language of human experience.

What story will your table tell? What legacy will you weave into its grain?

Join us. Add your voice. Transform a simple piece of furniture into a testament of the human spirit.

Founder of Intentional Table, international TEDx Speaker, author, and curator of transformative stories, Dr. Zoe-Ann Bartlett is passionate about partnering with influential brands, leaders, and filmmakers who want to give a voice to stories that ignite positive change. To learn more about Zoe, visit intentionaltable.com and follow her @intentionaltable.

Our Voices: Shape Optimal Healthcare Journeys Through Advocacy

by Lidia Molinara

I was lying in bed one night when a sudden, searing pain relentlessly tore through my upper abdomen. Each breath felt like shards of glass scraping against my insides, a sensation so painful it made me wince in pain. It was clear that this harrowing pain was not a passing discomfort. I knew I had to wake my parents so that I could go to the emergency room, despite it being 3 a.m. on Christmas Day.

In the hospital emergency room, I waited for hours, with no ability to even sit or stand because of the agonizing pain. We finally saw the emergency doctor, but he dismissed the pain as heartburn due to a larger-than-normal holiday meal. He provided a drink called a Pink Lady, which was a mixture of lidocaine, a pain blocker, and Maalox, an antacid, and I was sent home.

Back at home and still in the same amount of pain, I felt unseen, unheard, and helpless. I racked my brain, wondering what could be wrong. As a fourth-year pharmacy student, I thought it didn't fit any classic symptoms of appendicitis, pancreatitis, or gallbladder disease as the norm for that is classified as "forty, female and fat." Yes, this is what they taught us at the time!

I made a total of seven emergency trips over 90 days, and my body was withering away. At 5' 4", I weighed a mere 80 lbs., surviving on only water and bread. Each cycle of pain became an unwelcome 7-8 hours of lying in bed, holding a wet cloth to my head, and waiting for the time and extreme pain to pass. I would drink Maalox and then vomit into the sink right after because of the terrible taste. It would be so bad that I couldn't take it any longer, and eventually, I would end up in the emergency room again, waiting for hours and going through the same rinse-and-repeat cycle. It was only ever a diagnosis of heartburn and a Pink Lady solution that did not help.

The cycle of misdiagnosis and misunderstanding weighed heavily with each emergency visit, enduring the feeling of being a mere statistic in the system.

I became extremely frustrated. I refused to be pacified by "Pink Lady" medication solutions any longer. As a soon-to-be healthcare professional, I thought doctors knew best, that it wasn't possible they could misdiagnose. But the repeated attempts to seek answers that did not resolve my issue clearly meant this was simply not true, and I found my strength, a resolve to advocate for myself.

While I was in one of my many excruciating episodes of pain, I asked my mom to please drive me to my family doctor. Without an appointment, and with *barely* the ability to walk into the office, I requested to be seen.

Once the doctor came into the room and saw me, he advised, "Go to the emergency room and demand an ultrasound immediately!"

On my seventh emergency visit, I was hardly able to take a breath to speak. I told the triage nurse, "I am in 1,000 out of 10 pain, and it has been like this for over eight hours!"

I presented my written documentation of my health situation and explained that I had just left my family doctor, and he had told me to get an ultrasound immediately.

The nurse personally helped me into a wheelchair and wheeled me into an emergency room to be seen by the doctor. When the doctor came into the room this time, I actively engaged and reiterated what I had explained to the nurse. I presented my journal, showing how many times I'd gone through this pain, and demanded an appropriate painkiller while I waited to have an ultrasound.

I realized that my voice spoke volumes.

The emergency doctor did not give me a Pink Lady this time. He ordered a narcotic painkiller, and within two hours, I could actually breathe. I knew from my pharmacy studies that the painkiller he gave me helped with gallbladder duct spasms, so I concluded that he thought I had gallstones passing through me. He also ordered bloodwork to check my liver enzymes. Once I felt better enough to engage, when he came back to check on me, I spoke to him about the possibility of it being gallstones, and he simply said, "I can't believe no one had done an ultrasound yet."

The very next day, I was in surgery to remove my gallbladder after the ultrasound showed that my gallbladder was full of gallstones. I was lucky that I didn't get an infection or display any issues with my liver, as these complications can occur.

The invalidation I felt propelled me to spread awareness of how this experience taught me to navigate the healthcare system so that we could all be seen.

I learned the three key principles that make up the acronym ACE:

Advocate
Communicate
Educate.

I further learned that symptoms are not always clear, and the inability to diagnose can often be met with dismissiveness—this notion of "it's nothing to worry about, and it will pass." Therefore, it is extremely important to track and record your symptoms and to advocate your concerns. If you are feeling dismissed, the best approach to take is to communicate.

Here are three simple questions you can ask:

"I'm wondering, how should I cope with this pain, and when should I come back to be re-evaluated if things get worse?"

"Are there any other tests that can be done to try to get to a more definitive answer as to why I don't feel like myself?"

"When should these symptoms go away, or when will I feel better based on the treatment plan you outlined?"

When there is not a clear-cut diagnosis, sometimes it is a waiting game to see what happens, but you'll want to be clear on when you should follow up and where you should access that care: Should you go to the hospital? An urgent care clinic? The doctor's office?

Or just take an over-the-counter or prescription medication to help?

The primary healthcare professional should provide you with a treatment strategy, and if the issue hasn't been diagnosed yet, remember to continually seek answers and ask about what tests, medications, or labs could help lead to a diagnosis.

In addition, as caregivers, we often prioritize caregiving for our families over our own healthcare needs, neglecting preventative screening, symptom documentation, and follow-ups. We also need to make time to take an active role in our healthcare and advocate for ourselves in all healthcare encounters. We do need to do our research from credible sources, pay attention to these important dates, schedule the follow-ups, and go to these appointments.

It is difficult, since it can be disheartening to be told that nothing is wrong when you feel like there is an issue and it's not resolving. Again, I would have the treatment plan outlined by asking what you need to do to "be seen," essentially.

If you are not being seen or heard despite you asking the questions and trying to seek answers, then, if possible, I recommend you seek another opinion. This is also a way to manage the situation. In my case, it was when I went to see the family doctor as my second opinion. He gave me the insight to ask for an ultrasound, and that helped my diagnosis.

We also need to think of it as asking another friend for their opinion. It isn't "going behind your primary caregiver's back," but rather seeking more information. I have also seen clients get three opinions, and at times they can all be conflicting, so this is where the importance of trusting your instinct and doing your research can help guide you to the best decision for your situation.

Use your pharmacist as a resource as well. They are a wealth of information and a front-line accessible healthcare professional. It can be overwhelming, but feeling unwell is not a fun place to be, so do your best to seek answers.

After finding an opinion, try the treatment plan and see how you do. Not every plan produces results as expected, so it really becomes a trial-and-error situation, and it can be time-consuming and frustrating. Time also produces more clues, so it is important to monitor, track and record opinions, signs, and symptoms. This process helps with getting closer to a diagnosis, and it is also important in preventing errors.

Having dealt with my own healthcare ordeal, I realized that, across the globe, we face significant challenges in healthcare errors and medication mishaps. We are often taught that raising our voice in healthcare is wrong, but we have to shift this perspective. It is the very thing that will save and protect, and it's a necessity. It's not challenging authority; it's establishing your concerns.

Errors such as misdiagnosis are a segment of the things that can go wrong when seeking healthcare. The World Health Organization actively promotes World Safety Day to raise awareness of preventable errors in healthcare.

The most common errors occur with medications. According to the World Health Organization, there are over 3 million deaths a year from medical errors, and 50 percent of these are caused by preventable errors. Those medication errors are the highest number of preventable errors. It is extremely important to understand the medication treatment plan:

- How to take medications correctly
- What to avoid with them
- Their side effects
- When you need to go back and seek medical attention
- The name of the medication being prescribed
- The strength
- The directions
- The duration of therapy

When you go to the pharmacy, you can confirm that the pharmacist has given you the correct medication and it matches with what you were told by the prescriber. Also, it is so important to tell your pharmacist about any other medications you take, such as over-the-counter medications, herbal products, supplements, or illicit substances. These products can interact with prescription medication.

When picking up your prescriptions, confirm with the pharmacist how to use the medication. If you have allergies, ask, "Will this be a problem with my allergies?" (And be sure to name the allergy, i.e., my penicillin allergy.) This helps to make sure that no one has missed the allergy interaction. It will also be helpful to check online to confirm that you know even before you get to the pharmacy if the medication will create an issue.

Be honest. If you are not taking medication, then express this; this way, the treatment plan can reflect exactly your health situation and prevent additional tests, more prescribed medications, and further misdiagnosis.

As I embarked on my role as a pharmacist, I vowed I would hear the voices of my patients who felt muffled and help to empower them with the knowledge of ACE.

Let's go through ACE:

When you advocate, you remove the barriers so that you can speak up, lean into your intuition, voice your concerns, and push for answers.

When you communicate, you provide clear reporting of your health situation, you record, track, and keep accurate health records, and you present those in a truthful, clear, and concise manner.

When you educate, you learn more about the treatment plan, you do your research from credible sources, you develop questions from your research, and you ask them. You understand the risk vs. benefit of the treatment plan, and you follow up and check to make sure the plan is delivered correctly, is working, and is monitored.

Some simple ways to practice ACE are:

- Bring a pen and notebook to every healthcare encounter.
- Have your personal health history documented, including your family history, vaccine history, your reactions and dates of immunization, allergies to medications (and foods, especially peanuts), past medications and reasons if any were stopped, past surgeries with dates, current medications, herbal products and supplements you are taking, with doses and any other relevant health information

- Record your signs and symptoms, including dates and severity, to effectively communicate what you are experiencing. Be sure to also record your questions so that when you encounter the healthcare professionals, you remember what to ask!
- Track your screening and follow-up dates, and make it a priority to get to these appointments.
- Document what the doctor explains to you. Research the information, reference it with other providers to make sure your plan is carried out properly, and if needed, go back and ask further questions

In my TEDx talk, my speech at the United Nations, and my Take Care with Meds podcast, I spread awareness by outlining examples of how others struggled and the solutions they used to help prevent errors.

Healthcare is complicated, but it can be navigated. I encourage you to be vigilant by using ACE.

After all, when most vulnerable and in need of healthcare, we must be allowed to use our voices and be heard to protect ourselves.

The founder of the Take Care with Meds podcast and a speaker at TEDx and the United Nations, Lidia Molinara is an award-winning clinical pharmacist leader and certified geriatric practitioner. She champions patient engagement and empowerment to protect against medical errors and medication mishaps. Learn more at lidiamolinara.com and follow her @lidiamolinara.

Suicide Prevention: How to Be a SAFE Person and S.A.V.E. Lives

by Dr. Elayna Fernández

I'm done.
I can't do this anymore.
This is just too much.
What's the point?
Everyone's better off without me.
I'm better off dead.

I was lying in bed, sleepless, looking up at the rusted tin ceiling, when these thoughts showed up uninvited. I was only five years old.

The bruises, scratches, and stitches hurt, but not as much as the words I would hear every day. I couldn't quite articulate it then, but I can now. It feels like I am a living mistake making mistakes.

Eventually, my passive suicidal thoughts became active. I started to look around and fantasize about creative ways that would "get the job done."

School was my temporary haven, where people didn't act like I was a waste of space, where I was a teacher's pet, and where I could act out and feel powerful.

But even when I played with my friends at recess, I would think of death.

Who on earth thought it was a good idea to invent a game where a group of kids slowly witness the death of a human by hanging?

A couple of years later, I also read in the Bible that this is how Judas dealt with his guilt. I was convinced that if my own family thought I was "a spawn of the devil," and that I "should have rotten in my mom's womb," then I surely belonged on that tree branch, hanging out with Judas—in the literal sense.

But this wouldn't work. I lived in a small hut, and the rooms were only divided by makeshift curtains. I also never had a moment to myself. I was always doing some type of chore that I couldn't get right. It had to be something less conspicuous.

When I saw the dead rats on the landfill right behind our home in the slum, I thought I had found my saving grace. If the adults were so afraid of the children being around Tres Pasitos, the toxic powder that made the mice and the rats drop dead instantly, then it would probably be effective in putting me out of my misery. Tres Pasitos—three little steps. Sounded easy enough.

Death by poison worked for Romeo. I found confirmation in the peace and silence of the library as well.

The only way I could survive these thoughts was by writing about them until I collapsed. I wrote them in the blank spaces of my

Bible… as if to cry out to God in prayer that they would come true. But my heart would sink when I'd open my eyes early in the morning and find I was still alive.

Whenever I tried to talk about my feelings or to reveal these thoughts to anyone, they were denied, dismissed, and down-played. I couldn't see any other way out.

At 13, I acted on these thoughts. The next day, lying in the hospital room, the first person I saw when I came back to conscious-ness said, "Oh, you're alive… you can't even do *that* right."

I recently shared about these experiences during my fifth TEDx talk and at the United Nations. The audience seemed aghast. You could hear a pin drop.

While most people would never say such cruel words to some-one who is in pain, the problem in many other cases is that most people don't know what to say—so they'd rather not talk about it.

For example, when I tell others I am a cancer survivor, their faces light up. They ask follow-up questions and almost jump for joy.

In contrast, when I share I am a multiple-time suicide survivor, there are two common reactions:

1. There's shock … and silence… followed up by a change of subject.
2. They use default—and lethal phrases like: *don't give up, it will get better, be grateful, count your blessings,* or *look at the brighter side of life.*

FEMpower: Transformational Stories of Women Thriving Against All Odds

What I've realized living through over four decades with both passive and active suicidal thoughts as my most loyal companions is that positivity is fuel to the stigma of suicidality.

Motivational shame, as I call it, makes us wrong for something that is not our fault. What well-meaning people recommend or prescribe doesn't work for us, so it reinforces the feeling that we are broken and alone. This poisonous positivity doesn't make us grateful or hopeful for the future. Instead, it adds to our sense of defeat.

This is why, for years, I lived trapped in my shame-induced solitary confinement, sometimes obsessively looking for a cure, sometimes desperately looking for a weapon.

I can't tell you how many times I went deeper into a downward spiral because I was unable to "positively think it or pray it away."

And this is a reality that someone you love might be silently struggling with.

As I write this, The World Health Organization (WHO) estimates more than 700,000 people die from suicide each year. When I spoke in India to exactly 700,000 people who attended the event, I was overwhelmed by the rows of people inside the ashram tent and gathered outside in the streets. It is not just a massive number—it represents real people, with real lives. And, it's estimated that 135 people are potentially impacted by a single suicide.

Suicide is the second leading cause of death for children, adolescents, and young adults worldwide. It's urgent, it's common, and it could happen to anyone. It's a global human issue, and it's everyone's problem.

Many suicides are preventable.

Evidence proves that trauma does not come from experiencing adversity, but from feeling alone in our hurt.

Dr. Peter Levine, author of several best-selling books on trauma, says, "Trauma is not what happens to us, but what we hold inside in the absence of an empathetic witness." Positivity can be the most unsympathetic style of communication, and this is especially true when it comes to someone whose wounds are invisible or whose pain is hard to understand.

In my research, I've confirmed what I learned from my lived experiences: The way we talk about suicide can make it easier or harder to access support when needed. We feel unsafe with people who truly love us because the words they use turn out to be harmful when they mean to be helpful.

I am grateful for the countless crisis counselors at 988.org with whom I have chatted over the years. They have helped me stay alive when I felt I couldn't do it on my own. Sometimes, just knowing I have someone to call or contact eases the urge to die. Not motivational shame.

Safe people save people.

I've been spreading awareness about sensitive, proactive, and respectful suicide language for over a decade now. It's not easy to share my lived experiences, but the more I talk about suicide in my keynotes, interviews, blog posts, books, and in the work I do with others as an advocate, the more it helps us shed the shame, lose the jarring judgment, and shatter the stigma.

FEMpower: Transformational Stories of Women Thriving Against All Odds

I have shared a lot with you here. However, if you watch my United Nations speech, you will notice that I left out many specific details and spoke in general terms. Research shows that public communication that includes a description of the suicide method or location can increase rates of suicide behavior and imitation of the method or location described. It's important to omit photos, videos, diagrams, or illustrations that show the suicide method or location.

There are five easy guidelines I'll share below that we can all follow to decriminalize and destigmatize the word suicide and the experience of suicide:

1. Let's avoid the word commit.

Think about the uses of the word commit: "commit adultery" or "commit murder." We are not criminals or sinners.

I am hopeful when I read studies that show that academic publication of the word "commit" has decreased by about 20% since 2000—but we have work to do in our daily interactions with each other.

The sensitive way to say this is "death by suicide," "suicide death," or "fatal suicide behavior."

2. Let's ban the word attempt:

Staying alive is not a failure, and let's not ever imply that suicide is a success.

Using words like "successful" or "completed" is damaging when we talk about acts of suicide. Is surviving not the best outcome? Why then should we say someone "failed" at dying?

Remember that time I heard I couldn't "do it right" at 13 years old? Besides trying to end the pain that led me to take those actions, I was now motivated to prove that person wrong—by dying successfully.

I have had hundreds, if not thousands, of conversations with survivors of suicidality who have shared similar experiences.

A helpful alternative you can use is "acting on suicidal thoughts," because that is, in fact, what it is.

3. Let's stop talking about "taking a life" or "killing oneself."

These phrases are insinuations that we're not thinking of others or that we don't value our lives, which is ignorant, inaccurate, and even insensitive.

We don't want to take life, end life, or "end it all." We are simply seeking to end our pain. You know how pain medication is called a "painkiller"? Pain is really the only thing we want to kill.

I remember sharing my thoughts with someone whom I thought was safe. She proceeded to give me this golden advice:

"Think of your beautiful daughters!"

I was puzzled. Why would she believe for a second that I didn't think of my own children?

As people living with suicidal thoughts, we are often accused of being selfish or ungrateful, and our character is erroneously judged. It's as if we think about suicide as a fun idea to hurt the people we love, when in reality, we feel like a burden and like a lost case and we think we'd be doing them a favor.

Pointing out what a good life we are living or how grateful we should be is counterproductive and dangerous.

There are many factors at play when it comes to suicide. We're lonely and afraid and feel like suicide might be the most viable solution to seemingly unsolvable problems and unbearable pain. Suicide is an option because we can't find any other options. We need better options.

4. Let's not label people as "suicidal."

When we say someone is suicidal, we are defining this as their identity. It's dehumanizing and reductionist. They are someone who is experiencing suicidal thoughts, or like in my case, a person living with thoughts of suicide.

I am a daughter, sister, mom, writer, and speaker who loves to support others, be in nature, enjoy movies and music, and who lives with suicidal thoughts. I am caring, dedicated, and resilient. I won't define myself as suicidal—I am more than that. *We* are more than that. We are whole, divine beings with limitless potential, contributing to our shared human experience.

During a suicide prevention training, I heard someone quote psychologist Sally Spencer-Thomas, Ph.D., saying that the litmus test for talking about suicide is to substitute the word "cancer" for the word "suicide" to see if the sentence still works and has a supportive connotation.

I've been in remission for several years now. When referring to me, would you say, Elayna committed cancer? Elayna attempted cancer? Elayna was cancerous?

Or if you think of someone you knew who unfortunately didn't survive, would you say it was a "successful cancer"? I feel horrified just writing it hypothetically.

Just like we say "cancer death" or "died of cancer," when it comes to suicide, we instead could say "suicide death," or "died of suicide."

About a year after I wrote and published my first poetry book, I trained as a practitioner with the IFS Institute, and I got access to research and a body of work that confirmed what I had known intuitively. There are parts inside each of us, working hard to protect us in different ways.

I wasn't all cancer. I wasn't cancerous. A small part of me had cancer. We are not suicidal—we have suicidal parts.

Throughout my life, I have given my suicidal parts a voice through poetry. Carving out that safe space was an act of radical acceptance and a step toward becoming a safe person to myself.

5. Let's be sensitive and supportive.

Overall, there is no perfect way to talk about it, and the only wrong thing to do is to ignore admissions of suicidal ideation and/or behavior or to avoid conversations, especially because you are worried you might say the wrong thing.

However, there's an acronym I developed to learn—and remember—how to have a potentially life-saving conversation with someone who shares their pain:

S - Stay calm. The person coming to you already feels like a burden, so do your best to be stoic as they share.

A - Attentively listen. I call this "the ministry of presence." It means to provide silence, safety, and space as they share.

V - Validate their experience. Acknowledge their experience as understandable, warranted, and justified. Use safe language and their love language to help rule out suicide as the only option out of hardship.

E - Express gratitude for their vulnerability. When we thank someone for trusting us with their vulnerability, it helps redefine what it means to be "mentally strong," to flip our societal expectation that being strong is about pretending you are fine. Strength is not about pretending you are fine—it's about being honest when you're not.

To be a safe person, you don't have to be a mental health expert. You can be with someone through their proverbial bridge until professional help comes.

48

By learning to be a safe person to ourselves and others, we can remove the stigma around suicidal thoughts, decrease the suicide rate, and help people stay alive, because they will be more likely to seek and access the right tools, resources, and safety plans. They no longer feel like they have to suffer in secret.

My intention in sharing these language guidelines is to advocate for safe conversations that send a loud blaring message from you: "Your pain is valid, and it matters to me. You deserve to be here. You are not alone."

In no way I would like to vilify those who are not yet using the safe terminology. Don't judge yourself for not doing what you didn't know to do. And even when we know about it, it takes time to make the shift.

My invitation to you is this: the next time someone shares that they are going through a hard time, don't be positive. Be present.

SAFE people SAVE people.

Together, we can change the way the world perceives and treats people facing suicide.

And to those who, like me, face these thoughts one day at a time, I share my firm witness… it's okay to dance with death. Just make sure you take the lead.

Founder of the Positive MOM®, Dr. Elayna Fernández is a best-selling author, award-winning storyteller, and globally acclaimed speaker and media personality. She helps impact-centered leaders craft, tell, and use their stories to empower people to break cycles, find peace, and feel whole. Learn more at thepositivemom.com/ef and @thepositivemom.

How to Find Strength For Every Struggle and Season In Motherhood

by Mirella Acebo

I didn't hear my phone ringing in my backpack at first. When I finally pulled it out, I saw the four missed calls, and my heart sank. I knew exactly who it was and what she was calling about. I called the number, and the voice on the other end confirmed my worst fear.

It was my mom's care nurse, and her words hit me like a punch in the gut. "I'm sorry to inform you, but your mom has passed away. Would you like to see her body one last time?"

I was stunned by the question and not sure how to answer it. I thought to myself, "Is this how I want to remember my mom? Do I want that image seared in my mind forever?"

I did, but in all honesty, this was the last thing I ever expected given where I was... Disneyland. The irony, right?

There I was, surrounded by people smiling and laughing, caught up in the magic of "The Happiest Place on Earth." Meanwhile, I was drowning in grief and guilt.

Tears welled up in my eyes as I stood outside the Disney Princess stage show. I should've been there with her, not here, enjoying myself.

I felt an emptiness and immense loss that even Disneyland's magic couldn't touch. All I could think about was the sterile, cold reality of my mom, my anchor, in her hospital room, alone, as I drove down to her nursing facility one last time.

I grew up in the '80s as a latchkey kid (children who came home to an empty house after school because our parents were still at work) in Los Angeles, California. In my case, it was my mom, a single mom and immigrant from Mexico with a sixth-grade education who didn't speak English.

Growing up, I watched her work menial jobs as she struggled with a variety of health issues throughout her life: diabetes, osteoporosis, breast cancer, a stroke, and eventually Parkinson's disease. It was a lot, and yet I watched her do it with an extraordinary amount of grace and faith and not ever a complaint. And I mean never. And now, the only parent I had ever known was gone.

In the weeks after she passed, reality began to settle in. As a new mom with two little ones, ages nine months and two years, I was overwhelmed by one question: how would I navigate motherhood without her? She'd already taught me the basics through her example—how to love, sacrifice, and calm a fussy baby with patience and gentleness. But I needed more. I longed for the emotional support and guidance only she could give. Who would show me the things only she knew? Who would be there to love my kids as their grandma?

Whenever I looked at my children, I wished they could know her the way I did—her kind eyes, smile, love, wisdom, and the sweet friendship we shared. She had been my biggest cheerleader my entire life, and now, I didn't know how to move forward. The one thing I did know was that I wanted to honor her life in the way I raised my own kids. I wanted to carry on her legacy. But how, when I felt so stuck in my grief?

One day, I found myself home alone with my thoughts, and it hit me: the reason I felt so alone was because, as much as my friends tried, they couldn't really understand what I was going through. My friends meant well, of course. They showed up in the best ways by bringing me food, listening, and just being there, but they hadn't lost a parent. They couldn't connect with the layers of pain I was feeling.

That's when I realized I needed help beyond my friend circle—not the kind of help the typical new mom needs, but something deeper and focused on my internal struggle with my many "mom emotions."

In my desperation, I did two things that were way out of my comfort zone. First, I admitted to myself and my husband that I needed help. And second, I joined a support group.

The support group met once a week at my home church, a 15-minute drive from my house. This faith-based program was designed specifically for people grieving a loved one, and I appreciated its structure. It ran for 13 weeks, with each session featuring a video, small group discussion, and personal study throughout the week, which helped me process my emotions in light of Scripture.

Every week followed the same routine: I'd leave my kids at home with my husband, and honestly, it felt like a little slice of freedom. Stepping out my front door, I left the chaos of motherhood behind and entered a space where it was safe to be brutally honest and totally vulnerable. Taking the risk to open up in front of strangers transformed my life in ways I'll never forget.

I remember the meetings well. I showed up weekly with my pen and workbook in hand, ready to take notes, journal, and reflect on my progress. We were encouraged to share our reflections and answers from our homework, but I liked that no one was ever forced. It simply felt like a gentle invitation to open up at my own pace.

At first, I wasn't sure what to say, so I tested the waters with something simple: "I have never lost someone this close to me before, except maybe a pet."

Well, that didn't feel so bad, I thought.

As the weeks went on, I opened up more and more. I shared that my grief didn't start the day my mom passed; it had started years earlier when I began to lose the healthy version of her. I talked about the challenges of being my mom's full-time caregiver and how, in the process, I felt like I was losing pieces of myself. I confessed feelings of jealousy and envy at the happy moms around me whose lives seemed perfect. Eventually, I even expressed my lingering "mom guilt"—the guilt I carried for not being there with her when she passed, as if somehow I had failed her.

Letting all of this out little by little was both scary and relieving— like I was finally shedding the heavy weight I had been carrying for so long. It felt like a small step toward healing, and it felt good.

Over the 13 weeks, I learned many valuable insights along the way that can benefit anyone going through grief. Here are three of them:

1) Grief isn't a straight path. It ebbs and flows, and that's okay.
2) Time alone doesn't heal pain and sadness—we have to work through it and process our emotions in healthy ways.
3) Grief isn't a sign of weakness; it's a sign of being human, and in time, we find joy again.

One moment that really stands out is when I came across a journal question that asked, "Have you had a discussion with the Lord about your thoughts and emotions?" It hit me hard because my answer was, "No. I never thought of asking." That was a brand new concept to me.

I was glad I could be raw and vulnerable in this support group. It felt incredibly freeing. What truly surprised me were the responses from others. Instead of judgment, I was met with compassion, hugs, encouragement, and prayers. The support was overwhelming but in the best possible way. This became a turning point for me because I realized this is what I needed all along—for people to feel with me, not try to fix me.

After the class ended, I decided I still needed connection and accountability, so I joined every group that would take me: mom groups, church groups, school groups, and even the choir—even though I had no business singing!

The women in all of these groups became my lifeline. We shared our lives and our stories; our highs and lows, struggles, and doubts. These very real conversations with other women helped me feel normal, validated, and less alone in my feelings. They connected me on a deeper level to our shared humanity. I started to become more compassionate and empathetic.

The beautiful thing is, I discovered it was a two-way street. As much as I gleaned from the older and wiser women, it turns out I also had wisdom to share that was valuable too. The more I shared, the stronger and more confident I became. It's a beautiful thing to not only encourage others but to be encouraged.

Whether you're a mom like me or not, we're all human, and we can all relate to the intensity of the many emotions we feel—not just grief and guilt like I felt, but sadness, overwhelm, frustration, and regret. Sometimes we feel all in one day!

Our emotions are real, and sometimes they're so big that they hijack our thoughts and pull us into a deep abyss where it feels like we're drowning in them. It's a lonely and often scary place to be.

So, what do we do when this happens? For me, the answer was to ACT. I use the acronym A.C.T. to demonstrate, which breaks down like this:

A: Admit you need help

Just like I had to finally admit I couldn't do this alone, maybe you do, too. It's so easy to get overwhelmed by our emotions, and honestly, to stay stuck in them when we choose to isolate ourselves. I bet many of you can relate to thinking you have to tackle life's struggles all by yourself, but here's what I learned: emotions are actually a gift—they help us connect with other people around us. They're our universal language and the most honest part of us because they don't lie. They deserve to be heard, understood, and embraced. Acknowledging our need for support is a courageous step toward healing. Seeking help—whether through friends, family, or even a support group—opens the door to growth and transformation in your life. Remember, you don't have to go through this alone!

C: Connect with a community

For me, that meant reaching out to my home church and signing up for a support group and a Bible study. There, God provided Scripture to ground me, a spiritual family to surround me, and His love to sustain me. For you, it might look different. Think of a community where you can openly share your joys and struggles—whether it's with a small group of close friends, a neighborhood group, or a group at a community center. There are also virtual groups or forums online that can help connect us with others going through something similar. The key is to find a safe space where you can express yourself, seek encouragement, and build genuine connections.

T: Talk to God

Talk to God about your emotions and trust Him with your pain. I never thought to do that before, but I found examples in the Bible where people poured out their hearts and souls in prayer. From Hannah's heartfelt plea for a child to Hagar's anguished cries in the wilderness, I saw that they laid bare their struggles before God. If they could trust Him with their deepest sorrows and hopes, so could I.

FEMpower: Transformational Stories of Women Thriving Against All Odds

You may also consider the value of expressing your feelings through journaling, talking to a friend, or even reflecting quietly in nature. Allow yourself to be honest about your struggles and pain. It's in that honesty that you can begin to find healing and growth, opening the door to deeper connections with yourself and others.

The A.C.T. acronym is a great framework to remember when you're struggling: Admit you need help, Connect with a community, and Trust God (or a trusted friend) with your emotions. Talk it out and get it out, is what I like to say.

Is this process easy? No. It's not easy to open up and expose our inner world of emotions, but it's how we start to heal. And it's not like our pain and hardship magically goes away. But it's through human connection that our emotions are validated and our spirits find comfort.

The truth is, God never intended for us to do life alone. He gives us a spiritual family, brothers and sisters in Christ, to hold us, comfort us, and point us back to His love.

Today, I'm a well-adjusted, emotionally confident, and resilient mom with two wonderful adult kids. It's been 20 years since my mom passed, and I've learned to embrace my emotions and the lessons they bring. It's what has led me to become a life coach and teaching leader at a global Christian ministry where, for over a decade, I've been helping women grow their faith and God-confidence so they can navigate life's challenges with greater strength, purpose, and peace.

As the best-selling author of a book for moms, I also address 10 common mom emotions we feel today, including mom guilt, overwhelm, worry, and loneliness, and I connect them to the inspiring stories of 10 Bible moms who likely felt them too.

I'm passionate about guiding women on their journey of spiritual growth, empowering them to embrace their many roles as wives, moms, and individuals with grace and confidence. I love reminding women they're never alone and sharing practical tools to navigate the emotional ups and downs of life with resilience and hope.

I invite you to step outside your comfort zone and reach out when you need support. It's okay to share your struggles and emotions with people you trust. Your journey, no matter how difficult, has the power to inspire others.

Let's come together and be real about how we feel, so we can heal—in the arms of a loving community.

FEMpower: Transformational Stories of Women Thriving Against All Odds

A best-selling author and certified life coach, Mirella Acebo has been a women's ministry leader and teacher for over 10 years, helping women grow in faith and God-confidence. As The Life Coach Mom, she supports Christian moms through the emotional ups and downs of motherhood. Learn more at mirellaacebo.com.

How to Create Happiness Through the Social Influences of Mental Health

by Dr. Julie Radlauer

Have you ever felt lonely? For some people, it's difficult to admit, but do you know one out of every three people experiences loneliness?

I asked this same question to some amazing women when we were having dinner recently. We had been laughing and talking about our lives and our current work when one of them asked me about my research.

I shared that I was focusing on the social influences of mental health and that most of my work was in social connection. She wanted to know more.

This was a group of educated, upper middle class and middle class, gainfully employed women. Every single one of them confessed that they feel lonely—often! That's eight out of eight women, many of whom are married, have children, are surrounded by family and friends, and they still feel lonely.

You can have people around you and still feel lonely; you can be lonely in a job, lonely in a marriage, even lonely at a party.

Some feel that loneliness is just an emotion, and we all feel different emotions at different times in our lives. However, experiencing loneliness regularly often leads to depression.

In fact, according to the Surgeon General of the United States, we are experiencing a loneliness epidemic, which is leading to our current mental health crisis.

Sadly, loneliness impacts both our physical and our mental health. When we lack community connections, we have a greater risk of heart disease, a greater risk of Alzheimer's and dementia, are more likely to experience depression and anxiety, and actually die earlier than people who are well-connected.

What's even worse is that loneliness impacts women and girls at a higher rate than it does the male population. Research demonstrates that women are twice as likely to suffer depression and twice as likely to have challenges in accessing quality health services. More than 1 in 4 girls say that they have seriously contemplated suicide.

For me, this loneliness stems back to my childhood as a latchkey kid, which meant letting myself into the house after school, fending for myself for dinners from the local convenience store, and having the responsibility to make important choices at a young age.

You see, my mom was a single mom working full-time as a nurse to support us. She worked very hard and was an important role model in my life. While it wasn't ideal to spend so many hours alone as a teen, I believe it taught me independence, how to solve problems on my own, and invaluable skills to connect with others to get my needs met.

Once out on my own, I became fascinated with the idea of being a support for others, which led me to the field of psychology. For many years, I have worked in the mental health space, utilizing formal mental health treatment services to try to support those struggling.

At the beginning of my career, I was excited to make an impact on children and families because my mom didn't have the support that she needed when she was raising me. I quickly realized that mental health treatment services like therapy, medication, or case management are great for stabilizing a crisis. But the problem is once the situation stabilizes and families that needed support are discharged from services, they are out there on their own. When our services do not include helping families get connected to ongoing support systems like extended family, faith, friends, and community, then families often have to return to treatment services for support. I found this frustrating because often within six months, people that were previously successful were once again in need of support.

Ultimately, through research, I began to realize that Western mental health practices need more equitable solutions that can be used by people of all genders, cultures, ages, and stages. And, I found that the more I talked to people about their mental health, the more I realized that loneliness and lack of support is a universal truth.

This led me to embark on a national research project where I conducted interviews, focus groups, and literature reviews, and the results all pointed in the same direction: People prefer to have their mental health needs met in a less formal way that speaks to their culture. Not all communities want to seek professional mental health treatment from someone who does not share their culture and upbringing.

The communities that I interviewed and the literature both pointed towards focusing on the social aspects of our lives that we can impact. I call these the social influences of mental health.

The social influences include social connection, social support, social capital, social media, and social inclusion.

Social Connections: Socially connected people experience a sense of belonging to a group and feel close to others (Berkeley University). Further, social connection is "the energy that exists between people when they feel seen, heard, and valued; when they can give and receive without judgment, and when they derive sustenance and strength from the relationship." (Brené Brown) Being socially connected is the experience of feeling close and connected to others. It involves feeling loved, cared for, and valued and forms the basis of our interpersonal relationships.

Having social connections in your life has been documented to improve your mental health. A good way to intentionally create connections is to list five people in your life with whom you could potentially connect to determine if you can get to know them better or spend more time with them. Choose one person on your list and reach out to make a plan to meet up or talk.

Social Support: The help, advice, and comfort that we receive from those with whom we have stable, positive relationships. It includes supportive relationships and access to social networks comprised of the following functions: emotional, tangible, informational, and companionship support.

Social support can either be actual or perceived support and includes reciprocity, mutuality, and equality. When you have social support, you can get through difficult challenges, resulting in better mental health.

Research demonstrates when you have 3-5 strong supportive ties, you have better mental health. One way in which you can *create* support is to identify someone from your family, friend group, workplace, or community who may *need* support (e.g., someone who is moving, a friend who is ill and can use a meal, or even a person who just needs someone to talk to). Reach out to that person and offer support. The theory of reciprocity states that when you do something nice for someone, they are more likely to support you when you have a need.

Social Capital: The structure of networks and collective resources within a community that individuals within that community can draw upon that will benefit them.

Social capital refers to the relationships among people who live and work in a particular society, enabling that society to function effectively. When you feel that you have a network of support or contribute to the support of others, you experience a sense of belonging to that community.

This sense of community connection and belonging positively influences mental health. A good way you can build social capital in your life is to identify an area of interest where you may want to get involved (a local garden club, a political party, a faith-based organization, a community activity, etc.). Connect with the group and give it a try. Make the commitment to attend three times before you decide if the group is for you.

Social Media: There are demonstrated connections between social media and mental health. Technically, the definition of social media includes the websites and applications that enable users to create and share content or to participate in social networking.

Because social media is so widely used, it is necessary to understand how to use this connection tool in a way that will promote better mental health individually and collectively.

Think about it—when we're not intentional about how we use social media, we are allowing an algorithm to dictate who we communicate with and what information we allow into our brains. To manage your social media in a way that *improves* your mental health, do an audit. Pay attention to what you are watching and how it makes you feel, how long you are spending on social media, and what you are choosing not to do while you are on social media.

Use your audit results to make changes: You can unfollow the things that make you feel sad or anxious (like the news) and choose to follow things that make you smile (like puppies or nature).

Social Inclusion: When all groups of people have the same rights, opportunities, access to resources, and benefits.

Addressing social inclusion acknowledges that historical inequalities exist and must be remedied through specific measures, with the recognition that this process should be participatory, collaborative, inclusive of differences, and affirming of personal agency. Focusing efforts to understand, advocate for, and commit to creating an equitable society improves both our individual—and ultimately collective—mental health.

There is so much research about altruism that demonstrates when we live in a fair and just society, a sense of safety is created, which improves overall mental health.

To begin incorporating social justice into your world, identify a cause that is near and dear to your heart or one that really gets you frustrated. Look for a local community group, non-profit organization, or civic organization that is focusing on this initiative and make a call to volunteer.

Utilizing the social influences is a great way to create action and take control of our mental health. I found that people want to address their mental health in ways that speak to their culture, gender, age, and interests, utilizing more informal support.

The cool thing is that having social influences in your life is a protective factor, meaning that if or when something bad happens, these influences will buffer the bad experience. The trouble is that many young people don't know how to connect.

Our society has gotten away from connection due to the smartphone, families moving away from each other, a decrease in community involvement like faith-based activity, and the health crisis in 2020 (though we were already moving away from connecting before then). Many of our young people need to learn how to connect, support others, manage their social media, and more.

Utilizing this research, I was able to create Project CONNECT for adults who work with youth and Be Socially Connected for youth experiencing loneliness, depression, anxiety, and isolation. These initiatives are designed to provide knowledge about the social influences of mental health and why we need to pay attention to these aspects of our lives. But more importantly, it teaches how to make tangible changes to behaviors that will impact your mental health today!

Women and girls who participate in the programs report that they have better mental health, feel empowered with the tools and activities, and want to share this knowledge with other women and girls. We are creating a movement of young connection ambassadors who will inform the next generation about how to address their mental health through their everyday actions. We are teaching girls the skills to lift each other up and how to fix each other's crowns.

Now, I'm proud to say I'm giving the world what I needed growing up. I'm a doctor of public health, a business owner, a wife, and a mother of three children. I've spoken at TEDx and at the United Nations about how we can address our mental health crisis of loneliness through science-based, tangible tools and actionable solutions.

I share my research about ways that we can learn these tools to support our own mental health as well as the mental health of those around us with mental health professionals, educational systems, college students, and leaders. I conduct research in this space and continue to identify ways to impact our youth and support their improved level of happiness.

I invite you to learn more about the social influences of mental health so that you can take control of your own level of happiness and support those around you to do the same.

Here's how you can get started right now: Pick up your phone and think of one person who may need a little support. Then, send them a message that says, "I'm just thinking about you, and I would love to connect…"

Collectively, we can change the narrative on mental health.

A leading expert on the social influences of mental health, Dr. Julie Radlauer is the best-selling author of "CONNECT - 100 Ways to Create Happiness in Your Life." An international keynote speaker, featured on TEDx, she speaks about creating equitable mental health practices. Learn more at collectivelyus.org and follow @collectively_us.

Three Reasons to Celebrate Your Scars and Live the Best Version of Yourself

by Dr. Jiyoung Jung

My earliest childhood memory is screaming and crying at people who were rushing to pour cold liquid over my body. I was five when I accidentally fell into a huge pot containing boiling water.

In the 1970s in Korea, there were poor safety regulations, so we lived in a multifamily house with a shared kitchen. That day, one of the residents boiled water in a big pot and left the door open and lid off. I was playing hide and seek with my little sister, crawling on the floor, when the accident happened. The memory I have was a part of my rescue: my parents, pouring alcohol over me and cutting me out of my clothes.

I was treated in the local clinic for a while, but my wound was not healing well. So, I was transferred and hospitalized at the burn specialty hospital. I can still smell the treatment room. A stainless steel bucket was filled with wet gauze and blood that was scraped from my wound for healing.

I also remember being home in bed with an IV in my arm. It took lots of time, pain, and money for me to survive, and it left me with a huge scar on my body.

No one in my family expected I would become a functional adult because of the severity of the injury. I was a horrible burn victim.

When I was about eight years old, my mean aunt looked into my eyes and told me, "You will never get married. When men see your scar, they will run away from you."

I stood up tall and replied in a sassy tone, "No worries! I will dump that kind of man before I get dumped!" I do not know where I got the courage from at that time, but I needed it constantly.

When I was in the first or second grade, I went to the hospital every two weeks to get scar treatments. One required the painful stretching out of the scar so it could accommodate the growth of my body. There was a small glass filled with clear liquid medicine. It would be placed upside down in an injector that looked exactly like a stapler. Four people had to hold my body to stabilize me over the hospital bed. I would get 30 injections at once without any type of anesthetic over my scar.

This treatment was so debilitating and horrifying that I could not even lift a finger afterward. My mom would give me a piggyback ride so I could go to school. I vividly remember my mom's footsteps as she walked across the big empty school grounds. She met my school teacher so I wouldn't be absent from school, and then she carried me home and took care of me.

Guess what? I got a perfect attendance award for the entire 12 years of school.

This was the foundation that allowed me to become who I am and grow up as a healthy and happy citizen who is now living the best version of my life.

When I was in my early 20's, I had the blessing to marry a loving husband. I was curious about what he would say when he saw my scar.

"It must be painful," he said with a frown that turned into a smile. "I thank God to save you so I could marry you."

I thought to myself, "I absolutely found the right one for me!"

Soon after we married, I became a mom of two beautiful daughters. Our whole family came to the United States for my husband's studies. However, the same year we landed in the U.S.A., Korea faced national bankruptcy, which dramatically limited our financial support. The exchange rate between the Korean won and the U.S. dollar tripled. That meant I had to find a way to live on 70% less money than I had been.

I remember I was invited to a church member's home. In their pantry, there were four dozen boxed juices. I thought she was rich because we could not afford to buy even one single juice box. However, with solid faith and gratitude, we were able to support our family during those days and to be happy in spite of the circumstances.

I was a stay-at-home mom until my daughter went to the first grade. It was a time to pursue a career that would be meaningful and useful to me and the community. I was a teacher in Korea, so I considered teaching in the U.S.

My husband, the only person who believed in me, recommended I become a dentist, which was a great idea to fulfill my purpose. At first, it didn't sound realistic because I did not have any money to put towards my education, I had two little girls who were very active in school and extracurricular activities, I had to help my husband to build a business, and I did not know how to get there. I had no mentor or advisor.

I bravely took the first step: I decided to start learning English through an ESL program at a community college at the age of 30. Surprisingly, one person's beliefs is enough for us to pursue our dreams. ESL class gave me the confidence to start taking core curriculum classes like English composition, history, government, and math in community colleges.

Sometimes, I was able to take only one class in a semester. My car became my mobile library. Many times, I studied while I was waiting for my kids' soccer practice, violin lessons, and other events. All I did was take one step at a time and did my best to complete one class and celebrate it.

10 years later, I was admitted to a dental school at the age of 40. I screamed with joy when I read the acceptance emails from dental schools. My husband cried, and we prayed together to thank God.

After graduation, I had a year of residency to expand my knowledge and skills, and then, I became an owner of the practice. Now, I am a general dentist who specializes in sleep, breathing, and craniofacial development to treat the whole body. I love my career. Most of all, my husband John and I celebrated our 30th anniversary this year. This is truly a great human experience.

My biggest joy has been being a grandma of my precious Emma. It is such a blessing to watch her grow and to be a significant part of her life. And I just had a brand new granddaughter, baby Claire. Another beautiful life! What an amazing gift God gave to me!

I love spending time serving a local church, building a community, and mentoring the next generation. My mean aunt would have never guessed that I would be honored to be a speaker on the TEDx stage and at the United Nations, and to love my life the way I do. I didn't let the scar define me—it gave me the strength to build all I have.

Do you have a scar that is holding you back? Is that a reminder of pain? Do you feel like you will never get over it? Or are you using your scars to hurt people and justify your behavior?

Although my scars were not something I bragged about or hid from others, as I grew up, they really did not bother me. I would never wear a bikini or shower in public, so only a few people knew about them.

I learned how to live with my scars. It was not a big deal for me to have them.

Now that I am over fifty, looking back on my life, I realize that our scars can have a special meaning.

My scar means a celebration of *Life*.

I could be dead. That is a true statement, not an exaggeration. I could also have severe disabilities. Instead, I am alive, and I am a functioning adult. It was a miracle and a grace of God.

How much money would you pay for the exchange of life? It is priceless. The life you and I have is priceless. Every day is a brand new day.

I remind myself of this when I see my dog "Bomi." Her name means spring in Korean. Spring is my favorite season because I am always amazed by the new life that is presented in nature. New leaves in trees, new flowers in my garden, and new ducklings in my community pond are just fascinating. During winter, there is no evidence of life in some plants. They look so dry and dead. In spring, they show up and declare the power of life. The breath you are taking is a miracle of life. Celebrate every breath.

My scar means a celebration of Beauty.

What is your definition of beauty? I do not care how this world defines beauty, especially for women. I declare that I am beautiful. My life is beautiful.

I am not saying my scar is beautiful. It is very ugly from the thigh to the upper trunk of my body. But it is still part of me. I am embracing it and dancing with it.

Look at your face in the mirror. Look at your ear closely. Isn't that shape interesting and unique? You know you cannot function properly without your ear.

How about the wrinkles in your face? Especially around your eyes and forehead. Can you see the trace of your life? All frowns, laughters, and deep thoughts tell their own story in your face.

We change all the time, whether we like it or not. We get to dance with changes. It can be a tango or a chacha. Sometimes, it is a slow dance like a waltz. We just need to find our rhythm and put a smile on our faces. That is the beauty of life, even a scar. Every living thing has beauty in it. Find the beauty in you. You are absolutely beautiful.

Most of all, my scar means a celebration of *Love.*

Do you ever doubt there's love in this world?

I would not be here without all the love I received from my family, friends, many doctors and nurses, and God. Especially the love of my mom, who committed to securing her little girl's future the best way she knew.

Every human is born with 100% dependency on caregivers. No one will survive without the endless care of someone in the first few years of life. Being alive means you are already loved so much. Yes, someone loved you this much—even if that someone is far from perfect.

People have asked me how it feels to be a grandma of a two-year-old. I say, "I feel like I just entered a universe that never existed before."

Emma is the first grandchild in her generation, so she gets all the attention and love from great-grandparents, grandparents, and many aunts and uncles.

From the very day of her birth, it has taken a village to raise this one child. My husband and I have a lifetime master plan on how we are going to support or spoil this precious child. I truly want to do everything she asks for if it is humanly possible. And I am willing to die for her. Of course, I feel the same way about Claire.

One day, pondering on this, I had a revelation: If I were a God and could do anything and everything, would I provide everything my granddaughter wants?

My answer was *absolutely not.* I would let her experience human life—not only joy, love, happiness, and fulfillment, but also sorrow, frustration, failure, and pain. She should have the opportunity to learn, grow, and understand life, herself, and others. I want her to be happy when others are happy and be sad when others are sad. Of course, I would be beside her and watch and cheer for her every moment of her life.

I hope she can share the pain when someone is going through a hard time, so that she can be an inspiration when someone is struggling with moving forward. That is a beautiful human life. I know it will be really hard to let her suffer, and I will still be silent, but I believe that is love.

Throughout our lives, we experience many people and events that are pleasant, painful, and everywhere in between. They have one purpose: to give us lessons, so we can learn and grow. During that process, we often experience pains that can leave scars.

My scar was a physical mark. I can see and feel those, but it is not painful anymore. Many scars are invisible—they can be mental and emotional, and they can be subconscious. So, many people may not even admit they are living with scars. Many people still feel pain or shame with their scars because they never heal properly.

What meaning are you giving to them? What story are you telling yourself?

If you are reading this, I believe you are one of the luckiest people on the planet. It means you are still alive, your heart is beating, you have enough education to read, you are physically capable of holding the book or device, or you have a loved one who reads it for you and you are able to hear, you have had a life event that led to this book, and you have a desire to read. Not many people have this opportunity. Your life is a love story despite your scars.

Our scars are a greater reminder to celebrate our life, beauty, and love.

I invite you to give any scar you might have a new meaning.

Take a deep breath. Think about what they bring to your life. I understand this may bring you painful memories at first. Think deeper. During your healing journey, your scar may lead to new people, a new environment, and a new opportunity. Your scar may make you more resilient, strong, and soft. They help you become who you are as a beautiful human.

You have the power to give meaning to a scar. You have the power to decide what name you call it. It is just like the power switch in your hand. Turn it on. So you can live the best version of yourself.

The CEO of Central Park Dental, Dr. Jiyoung Jung is an award-winning dentist and educator who has been named Best Dentist by D Magazine in Dallas. She has been featured on ABC, NBC, FOX, CBS, and stages such as TEDx and the United Nations. Learn more at centralparkdental.net and follow @doctorjjung.

How to Transform Your Timid Team Members Into Confident Powerhouses

by Mary Ottman

Looking at the bed I shared with my grandmother in our single-wide trailer in the country, I knew I would never have my friends over. Unlike them, I was a worldwide, bonafide trailer park kid!

At only 15, I was so embarrassed by my appearance. Sadly, I had inherited the gifts my family passed down to me. I didn't have straight teeth or a smooth complexion. I would hold my hand over my mouth when I laughed so no one could see my teeth.

When I looked in a mirror, I would feel a heavy knot of shame forming in my stomach. All I could see were my flaws.

Several different brands of foundation were lined up on my bathroom counter. I had tried them all, but none of them covered my problematic complexion. Sigh.

I felt so ashamed of my living conditions and my appearance, but I secretly clung to my dream that someday, someone would see beyond my imperfections and love me for who I was inside.

One day, I walked into class wearing my new skinny jeans. I felt so pretty. We were previously unable to afford them, and I was so excited to have a pair finally!

I leaned down to slide my books under my desk. When I sat back up, I couldn't believe it—the popular guy at school was sitting at the desk in front of me!

It felt like a magical fairytale moment...

I started thinking a million thoughts at once.

"What if this super cute guy talks to me? What should I say? I think he liked my new skinny jeans. No, that's stupid, because he would never go out with a nerdy girl like me. That is not why he sat there."

My heart was racing in my chest.

He slowly started to turn around and look at me. All the thoughts suddenly stopped, and I sat there like a deer caught in headlights.

He leaned towards me until his face was six inches from mine. Staring at him, holding my breath, I was paralyzed with disbelief. I had dreamed of this moment for so long.

He leaned in even closer and turned his head so his mouth was so close to my ear that I could hear his breath.

He paused for a few seconds and whispered, "What are those spots on your face?"

Then, with a look of disgust, he immediately turned back around. A huge, hot wave of shame washed over me.

"I'm not going to let him see me cry."

I tried to fight back the tears but felt them slowly rolling down my face. I quickly wiped them away, hoping no one had seen them.

I was devastated as the tiny amount of confidence I had slowly faded away.

I ugly cried myself to sleep for several nights. Then, finally, the sadness lifted, and I thought, "You know what? I don't have straight teeth, and I don't have clear skin. But what I do have is my brain, and my brain is my ticket out."

There was no way around it. I had to go to college to improve my life.

When the time came, with the support of my loving grandparents, I began applying for scholarships and eventually accepted one to a college located two hours away.

The night I said yes, my stomach churned like I was on a rollercoaster ride. One second, I felt excited to leave town. Then panic surged through me at the thought of living on my own. Then, my heart ached at the thought of leaving my family and friends behind.

But, as we say in Alabama, "there was nothing else to do but to do it."

That fall, I packed my things into my 1976 Chevette and headed out on I-24 to start my next chapter.

As much as I wanted to be there, college felt like a relentless journey of pain, struggle, and uncertainty. At one point, I juggled three jobs while attending classes just to make ends meet. My days were consumed by work and study, and I was utterly exhausted. Even so, it was absolutely worth the effort.

Five years later, the struggle paid off. I graduated and got a great job in the Army as an electrical engineer. I could finally go to a dermatologist and pay for my braces!

After that, when I looked in the mirror, I saw my reflection and felt a boost of confidence. I wish I could say that was all I needed to smoothly sail to the top, but that would be an epic lie.

No matter how hard I worked, or how highly I was rated by other leaders, I knew and could feel that my supervisor did not believe in my potential.

One time, he even told me men should make more money than women. "They have to sign up for the draft," he said with a smirk.

You're probably wondering, *did you stay?*

I did. Tragically, I spent those years trying to prove my worth to someone who would never acknowledge it.

Then, lucky for me, 15 long years later, he retired.

I was surprised to learn how different my new supervisor was. He would find something positive to say about everything I did. I could tell that he believed in my potential.

Unlike the temporary and outward confidence I got from finally getting braces and visiting the dermatologist, his encouragement helped me believe in myself and increase the inner confidence I needed to become the confident leader I am today.

His faith in me provided validation that I was good enough, smart enough, and ready to step out of my comfort zone.

And that's when everything changed. My career skyrocketed.

I applied and got leadership positions that allowed me to give value to my organization. Based on my results, I attended the Army Senior Service College, where Army leaders receive executive-level training.

Graduating from that program opened the door to the biggest break of my career. I was offered a position as Deputy Product Director in an outstanding organization known for its culture of innovation.

Their culture centered around supportive risk-taking, and I have to admit, each time I was asked to take on a bigger challenge, the negative voice in my head went wild.

"You're not ready for this. You don't know enough. There is no way you can do this. Everybody in this office is going to laugh at you. You are going to look so stupid."

With each passing negative thought, a wave of fear churned in the pit of my stomach. But I felt that fear, and I kept moving forward. Then, as we stretched for the big wins, I felt even more confident.

The experiences I gained while working there boosted my confidence exponentially. Sure, I encountered my share of failures, and I learned valuable lessons. I was also thrown into unfamiliar, high-stakes situations and handled them successfully.

For example, when my boss was suddenly sick and out of the office for six months with no notice, I had to take the reins immediately.

I began traveling constantly to meet with our contractors around the country and to brief senior leaders at the Pentagon.

Between the career development I had received and my growing wealth of experience, I was able to successfully defend our program to those senior leaders at the Pentagon, time and time again. And I went from the girl who never smiled to the confident leader who stands polished and ready to stand in front of a room full of reporters' microphones.

Today, this type of targeted training and support is exactly what employees want.

In fact, they don't just want it. They are leaving if they don't get it.

According to shrm.org (Ruehl) statistics, SHRM (Society for Human Resource Management) Annual Voluntary Turnover in 2023 was 23%.

This metric represents the average voluntary turnover rate in the United States across all industries. It's essential to recognize that turnover rates can vary significantly between different sectors.

The employees included in the Annual Voluntary Turnover statistic did not get fired or laid off. They left voluntarily for other reasons.

The challenge is to identify the cause of your organization's voluntary turnover. Some questions we can ask are:

- Which employees are leaving?
- Are they new employees or high performers?
- Why are they leaving?
- Is there any pattern you can see between who is leaving and when?

Some employees discover they do not feel aligned with the company's mission or values. Other employees leave for better job opportunities. Some leave because they do not feel they are getting the training and support they need to do their jobs.

I recently read a study conducted in 2023 by TalentLMS (a cloud-based learning management system) and Vyond (a cloud-based animated video creation platform) that found that if companies did not offer training opportunities, 41% of employees intended to seek new job opportunities in 2024 (Casic et al. 4).

Let me ask you a few other questions:

- Are your employees being provided the necessary training to successfully perform their job duties?

- Does your culture support and encourage having more experienced employees mentor newer people?
- Are employees leaving just before appraisal time?

Something to think about is that if several employees under the same supervisor leave your organization, it may indicate poor leadership. Thankfully, we now can train supervisors to provide the support that employees expect.

Another reason employees quit is because their supervisor has treated them poorly. As a leadership expert, I am trained in addressing toxic leadership behaviors and minimizing the likelihood of employees leaving due to mistreatment.

There are times when a toxic leader will dig in their heels and resist efforts to change. They may not see the need to change, even when faced with the negative outcomes of their leadership style.

Retraining leaders can be challenging, but toxic leadership harms businesses. In today's job market, your organization cannot afford to tolerate toxic leadership. And everyone on the team can use some positive reinforcement and encouragement.

Employees may also experience uncertainty or fear regarding potential layoffs. No one wants to be the last person to leave a sinking ship. Some feel that resigning at the first sign of trouble gives them the best chance of finding another job.

A recent ResumeTemplates.com survey stated that 40% of companies who participated in the survey will replace workers with artificial intelligence (AI) in 2025 ("4 in 10 Companies Will Replace Workers").

A great leader understands that employees are understandably anxious about job security. Offering training that enhances their skills and equips them for higher-level positions is essential.

If laid off, this training can boost their confidence in qualifying for other positions elsewhere. It may also increase their likelihood of staying if they continue to receive training, even though layoffs are possible.

I've quoted several statistics so far, but I'm about to share the one that poses a specific threat to your bottom line.

I found an August 2024 article on hubstaff.com (Whiting), which states that approximately 47% of HIGH performers left their jobs in 2022 alone. That's almost half.

But that's not all. The article also states that high performers are about 400% more effective than average employees. This type of turnover is a massive threat to your bottom line.

Do you have succession plans in place if half of your high performers walk out the door?

The bottom line is this: If you're not providing training and opportunities that build your employees' confidence and increase their skills, studies indicate that you are missing out, and you are impacting your bottom line.

Speaking of taking action and moving forward, I left my 27-year career as an executive leader in the Army to pursue my passion for helping others and to establish my speaking business. It gives me absolute joy to help others become confident, purposeful, and productive leaders.

Through my corporate leadership talks, workshops, and consulting, I help organizations transform their employees from those who lack confidence in speaking up to those who show up as confident powerhouses.

My new career has allowed me to travel, become an author, and experience things I never thought possible. I have spoken at the United Nations and received a Presidential Service Award. I'm still pinching myself!

The great news is that if I can go from the trailer park to the Pentagon, anyone can develop the confidence they need to advance their career!

I invite you to take one simple action step to help your employees become more confident. Think of an employee with potential who seems uncertain of their capabilities when asked to take on more responsibility. What actions can you take to encourage them? Block off time on your calendar and take that step. That's it! It's simple and effective.

If my new supervisor had not encouraged me, you probably would not be reading my chapter today. His belief in me was powerful, and even life-changing, in my case.

You have the same power to change your employees' lives when you believe in them. Show them that you do!

TEDx speaker, author, and professional leadership speaker Mary Ottman is an award-winning executive leader, certified leadership coach, and champion for your professional success. Mary provides corporate leadership talks and workshops that help aspiring and mid-level managers become unstoppable high-performance leaders. To learn more, visit maryottmanspeaks.com and follow her @themaryottman.

Five Strategies for Enhancing Reproductive Health and Personal Growth for Women

by Amb. Dr. Catherine Utsalo

What happened to my baby?

Who rejected whom?

Did the baby reject the mother, or did the mother reject the baby?

Whichever way it went, it didn't matter—first, it was the sharp pains, then tears, then blood, and the life that was developing inside of me melted away.

"Mama…" I screamed, holding on to myself.

I was terrified to tell my family that I was pregnant outside of wedlock. Yet, I felt joy knowing that I was carrying a child. I love children and had raised many, although they were not my biological children. I was truly joyful knowing I was carrying my own.

"As long as you are a woman, you are a mother." It is a natural thing. Only my boyfriend and a close friend knew, so I was secretly planning for my baby—if he was a boy, Emesomi, if she was a girl, Isomi.

By the third month, I tragically lost the pregnancy. This loss occurred before my family members ever knew about it, adding a layer of isolation and sorrow to an already difficult situation.

The pain of losing a child is indescribable, and it left me devastated. The emotional and physical agony was immense. It felt like a part of me had been torn away.

Just as I was grappling with this loss, the doctors delivered another blow: I had fibroids and needed surgery.

What causes fibroids? National and international doctors couldn't explain.

My mind raced faster than a rocket. I prayed and prayed and prayed; that is all I knew. I cried endlessly because I couldn't tell my family about the pregnancy, but I had to tell them about the fibroids. Feeling so much shame, I lost my self-esteem.

In the midst of all this, I faced another significant obstacle. The doctor treating me insisted that I undergo a hysterectomy, stating it was necessary due to heavy bleeding, episodes of fainting, and blood transfusions. When I refused, he told me I was not in compliance and discharged me. Even though I had just fainted, was iron deficient, and was still recovering, he sent me home.

I begged, cried, and argued that the fibroids could be removed without removing my womb, but he dismissed my concerns and sent me away. I was terrified yet calm.

Undeterred, I sought a second opinion. Another doctor reassured me that it was indeed possible to remove the fibroids (myomectomy) without removing my womb (hysterectomy). This validation was a turning point, reinforcing my belief in overcoming the obstacles before me.

Undergoing uterine fibroid surgery was a trying time, both physically and emotionally. But the real challenge lay in the recovery. The scars weren't just on my body but on my spirit as well. Each day was a battle against pain, doubt, and fear.

My boyfriend left me, which made people wonder what was wrong with me. Some people even mocked me, saying, "You're not good enough for a wife." They called me, "Sick, sick," as I went by, and other things I really don't want to mention because they are so humiliating and denigrating that I do not want to repeat them. They were unaware of the miscarriage I had suffered before the fibroid surgery, and since others didn't know about the miscarriage, I couldn't talk about it or begin to heal properly.

I felt broken, and although I was in desperate need of help and emotional support, I felt unable to reach out.

Because of my faith, I began to see my challenges as a path to rebirth. I started focusing on my personal growth, on becoming a better person despite the hardships.

I began educating myself about fibroids, their causes, and possible solutions. I sought advice from others who had gone through similar experiences. I received support from some friends and family members. This journey of learning and support empowered me to take control of my health and healing.

FEMpower: Transformational Stories of Women Thriving Against All Odds

Faith played a central role in my transformation. Through prayer and meditation, I found strength and resilience. I came to understand that forgiveness was essential—not just for others who might have wronged me, but for myself.

I also discovered that nutrition and lifestyle changes could support my healing journey. Incorporating nutrient-rich foods, regular physical activity, and stress management practices helped me regain my strength and improve my well-being.

Most importantly, I chose to forgive myself for the loss of my child and the perceived failures that had weighed me down.

My experience taught me that the emotional and psychological scars of reproductive health challenges can be as significant as the physical ones.

During my recovery, I lived in constant fear, especially during my monthly periods, haunted by the trauma of heavy bleeding in the past. Nights were filled with anxiety, waking up thinking I had soaked the bed, only to realize my menses were now normal.

This fear drove me into an unhealthy, overly strict diet, desperate to avoid a recurrence of fibroids. Even the thought of relationships became daunting—I feared rejection and struggled with the vulnerability of sharing my surgical history.

This journey showed me the importance of addressing both the physical and emotional aspects of recovery and supporting women through their healing processes.

Today, I am thriving, free from fibroids, and filled with a deep trust in God. I prioritize self-care and self-love, making time to nurture my mind, body, and spirit.

The rejections I faced no longer define me; they have refined me. They have made me more compassionate, more determined, and more resilient. As an ambassador to the United Nations, I am using my trauma to advocate for the rights and well-being of women and girls. In addition, I am an information technology consultant (IT) and a gospel singer. I hold herbal and holistic wellness certifications and am pursuing a PhD in psychology and Christian counseling. I also share insights on cultivating self-worth and empowerment as an author.

I run a program called "Mothers are First Responders: Fibroids Begone." Through this program, I aim to ensure that no woman has to endure the pain and isolation I faced alone. We provide free CPR/ First Aid/ Child care training, and ultrasound services, educate women on fibroids, assist with surgery costs, and offer free menstrual hygiene training when distributing sanitary pads.

I believe there are five determining factors to combat stigma and ensure optimal reproductive health for every woman to thrive:

1. Provide a Community for Early Support

A supportive community enables women to discuss reproductive health without fear or shame. Safe spaces allow women to openly talk about issues like menstrual health, fibroids, miscarriages, and infertility, leading to early diagnosis, better treatment, and emotional healing.

With the support of a network, women gain the confidence to seek medical attention sooner, breaking down the stigma that often surrounds these issues. Encourage dialogues about reproductive health in schools, workplaces, and communities. Develop campaigns that normalize discussions on menstrual health, fertility challenges, and reproductive conditions.

When women join support groups, they gain insight and support from others with similar experiences. Family support plays a crucial role in helping women navigate the challenges of reproductive health issues. A strong support system within the family can offer emotional stability, provide practical assistance during medical treatments, and reduce feelings of isolation.

Encouraging open communication and empathy within families fosters a nurturing environment, empowering women to manage their health with confidence and strength. Family involvement can also advocate for better healthcare access and education, benefiting women suffering from reproductive health challenges.

2. Enhance Access to Medical Care

Many women face barriers such as limited healthcare facilities, lack of insurance, or financial constraints. Improving access to healthcare, including screenings, ultrasounds, and routine checkups, helps women manage their reproductive health effectively.

Additionally, ensuring access to menstrual hygiene products is vital, particularly for young girls in underserved areas.

Through our "Mothers are First Responders: Fibroids Begone" network and program, we provide free CPR/First Aid training, equipping women with life-saving skills that support family and community well-being.

Menstrual hygiene education and distribution of free sanitary pads empower girls with knowledge and resources for menstrual health.

Support for women to access free ultrasounds and fibroid surgery assistance helps women obtain vital screenings and treatment for better reproductive health.

Some solutions I suggest are implementing mobile clinics to reach women in rural or underserved areas, and offering services like reproductive health screenings, prenatal care, and general check-ups without the need for long travel.

Another way to increase care access is by expanding access to telemedicine, enabling women to consult healthcare profession-als remotely for advice, prescriptions, and follow-up care, and reducing barriers such as distance, time, and cost.

I also recommend creating low-cost or subsidized health insur-ance options that cater specifically to women's health needs, including coverage for maternal health, contraception, and reg-ular screenings. This is another way to ensure that financial con-straints do not prevent access to necessary medical care.

Empowering women with knowledge to make informed deci-sions about their reproductive health can be transformative. This includes understanding anatomy and menstrual hygiene, and recognizing symptoms of potential conditions like fibroids or endometriosis.

3. Education

Becoming and staying informed is essential to advocating for oneself. When faced with a possible hysterectomy, I researched alternative treatments and options. In the same way, knowledge equips women to have meaningful conversations with doctors and make informed decisions.

However, reliable sources are crucial to avoid misinformation. Listening to one's gut feelings is invaluable in healthcare. My own instincts led me to seek alternatives when the first doctor suggested a hysterectomy.

All women should feel empowered to question medical advice and seek alternatives when needed. Being proactive in healthcare decisions ensures that the chosen treatment aligns with personal goals.

4. Financial Assistance

Many women, especially in underserved communities, face financial barriers that prevent them from accessing essential medical services, which causes them to delay necessary care due to financial strain.

Women should have access to health loans with minimal credit check requirements to ensure equitable healthcare opportunities.

By simplifying credit checks and focusing on their genuine needs rather than stringent financial criteria, we can empower women to prioritize their health and well-being. This approach not only supports their individual growth but also strengthens families and communities, fostering a healthier and more inclusive society.

I also believe there should be access to education and career advancement for women to elevate women from poverty. That's why we offer childcare training and provide IT training to women through my organization, under our program called "Creating IT Career Awareness Amongst Women." This program empowers them with skills for better career opportunities and higher earning potential. Our programs focus on bridging the digital divide, equipping women with the tools needed to thrive in today's tech-driven world.

5. Forgiveness as a Path to Healing

Forgiveness is a powerful and often overlooked aspect of healing, especially in the context of mental and physical health. Holding onto pain—whether from loss, societal pressure, or personal challenges—can have a profound effect on our well-being, leading to chronic stress, anxiety, and even hormonal imbalances.

As a forgiveness coach and a PhD candidate in psychology and Christian counseling, I focus on helping women recognize the healing power of letting go of past hurts. I teach women who choose to rise from the ashes of rejection and pain all. It all boils down to forgiving others and forgiving ourselves for our well-being, emerging stronger and more confident.

It's been said that unforgiveness is like drinking poison and expecting the enemy to die—it only harms the one holding onto it.

Forgiveness not only eases emotional pain but can also improve reproductive health by reducing stress-related hormone fluctuations. Our not-for-profit organization offers coaching sessions in Forgiveness for Well-being, where women can learn to release emotional burdens and embrace healing.

By cultivating a mindset of forgiveness, women can reclaim their health, peace of mind, and sense of inner strength. It's a vital step toward breaking free from past trauma and embracing a future of personal growth and empowerment.

Ultimately, learning to forgive oneself and others creates space for physical and emotional recovery, fostering peace and helping the body heal. It allows women to reclaim their strength and move forward with confidence.

I want to leave you with this message: Our worth is not defined by others' judgments or by the challenges we face. It is defined by how we respond to them, by our resilience, and our determination to rise.

My name in my language is Agionomoisi Orkotsenonomoh. It means, "You don't laugh at those who are blessed." I am blessed to be a blessing. I am a child of God, Jesus lives in me, and Jesus shines through me.

I know that as we end the secrecy and stigma and decide to be a blessing to help women become healthier, we bless the whole world.

I stand before you in victory, and I invite you to support organizations that are helping make that a reality.

S.T.O.R.Y. Compiled by Dr. Elayna Fernández

Join us on our mission to empower women and break the silence around reproductive health. Together, we can create a world where every woman has access to the care, education, and support she deserves. Let's build stronger communities, lift women out of adversity, and embrace forgiveness as a path to healing and well-being.

Trust your instincts—if something doesn't feel right, seek clarification or alternative opinions.

Ask about all treatment options, including non-invasive procedures, and the risks and benefits of each.

Remember that you have the right to choose the treatment that best suits your health needs.

Your voice, your actions, and your support can make a lasting impact. Be part of this movement for change, and help women thrive!

Philanthropist, pastor, gospel singer, and certified IT consultant, Amb. Dr. Catherine Utsalo is a forgiveness coach, speaker, author, and founder of "Mothers are First Responders," CEO of Moisi Naturals, and vice president of Prezens for Charity. Follow her on Instagram @moisi_naturals, @moisi_praise, and Facebook at Prezens for Charity.

One Tool to End the Stigma of Hair Loss

by Stephanie L. Anderson

The Consultation

I saw her walk nervously through the door, ready for her consultation at the hair restoration center with me that day. As I reviewed her new client questionnaire, I began to ask her a few questions to break the ice. Because there was no visible loss of hair, I asked, "How can I be of service to you?"

In my 30 years in the hair industry and as a practicing trichologist and hair loss professional, I've found some clients believe that "early is on time, on time is late, and late is unacceptable!" I assumed Celeste was one of those clients. (Not her real name.)

Looking me in the eye, she said, "I found a small lump during my monthly breast exam." In that moment of shock for me, I strangely felt her nervousness begin to dissipate. Celeste said, "Ms. Anderson, I have come to peace with having breast cancer. I am hopeful about the course of treatment I will be undergoing."

I listened with intention and watched a tear fall down her cheek.

"Do you know what the hardest part of it is?" she asked.

As I handed her a tissue, I was at a loss for words.

"The hardest part is not having my breast removed. The hardest part is losing my hair," she stated sadly.

Even though Celeste's words impacted me to the core at the time, this was a sentiment that countless clients would express in the following decade of serving those losing their hair. Chemotherapy is not the only cause of hair loss. Stress, trauma, immune system disorders, in addition to chemotherapy can all be factors.

As with other challenges in life, the fear of alopecia (a general term for the loss or absence of hair from the body), the worry over the *when* and *if* it's going to happen, doesn't have to control your life.

Impact of Social Stigma

In my research, I found that alopecia is one of the side effects of chemotherapy that patients fear most; to the point that, just for that reason, up to 14% of women refuse chemotherapy. Chemotherapy drugs destroy rapidly growing cancer cells but do not spare other rapidly growing cells, including hair keratinocytes. This means the chemotherapy drugs cannot distinguish which rapidly growing cells to destroy, leaving hair cells vulnerable.

I find myself in unique and heart-wrenching situations when clients like Celeste walk through my door. You see, until her diagnosis, she had never imagined losing her hair. Vibrant and full of life, her hair had always been a source of pride. The thought of hair loss as a result of cancer treatments, or chemotherapy-induced alopecia (CIA), hit her like a freight train. It was devastating. Unfortunately, Celeste is not alone in this fear; it's a common and real concern for many people facing a similar journey.

What was your first thought reading that up to 14% of women refuse treatment just to avoid the side effects of losing their hair?

This statistic speaks volumes about the pervasive social stigma surrounding hair loss and its psychological implications. Hair holds immense power in our society, which is why it can symbolize beauty, femininity, and even identity. For many women, losing their hair can feel like losing a part of themselves—a scary prospect that can lead to a crisis of self-image.

In our initial conversation, Celeste opened up about her fears with emotional candor. "I just don't think I can handle people staring at me," she said, her voice quivering with anxiety.

Moments like these remind me of how deeply intertwined our emotions are with our appearance. Hair is more than just strands on our heads; it can represent confidence, social standing, and even cultural identity. Once hair starts to thin or fall out, the ripple effects can go far beyond physical appearance.

But let me reassure anyone struggling with these fears: you are not alone. Hair loss due to chemotherapy is a common side effect that impacts many women, and it typically affects their emotional well-being and self-esteem. The feelings of anxiety, dread, and even despair that accompany the diagnosis of cancer are compounded by the worry about their hair. It seems unfair, doesn't it?

They are already facing a life-threatening disease, and now they must grapple with this additional fear of losing their hair, too.

One of the hardest conversations I often have with clients is about the social perceptions of hair loss—how society sometimes discounts the emotional labor that accompanies it. I remind my clients that the conversations we have regarding beauty standards are flawed. Those unrealistic ideals can leave us feeling even more isolated when we are in a vulnerable state.

With Celeste, we spent time discussing her hair and her identity. I guided her through the various options available to manage the CIA, from preventative treatments to alternatives such as wigs or scarves that could help her maintain a sense of normalcy. I encouraged her to explore styles that would make her feel empowered, even if she did lose her hair. Many clients find solace and confidence in selecting a beautiful wig that matches their personality, while others opt to embrace their baldness. For both, each choice can elevate their mood and help them maintain a sense of self, even amidst uncertainty.

It's crucial to acknowledge that while cancer treatment may cause hair loss, it is temporary. For many, this is a significant source of comfort. When the treatment ends, hair typically regrows, often with a different texture or color than before. Although my specialty most often has more women clients seeking my services, this can apply to men as well. However, the journey can feel daunting when someone is in the thick of it; it's easy to forget that these changes are not permanent.

As part of my role, I emphasize self-care techniques that can help clients manage the emotional turbulence associated with both temporary and permanent hair loss. This includes affirmations, mindfulness practices, journaling, and joining support groups that focus on both emotional and psychological support for those going through similar experiences. These modalities help my clients connect, share their feelings, and reduce the emotional weight of their fears.

I often remind my clients that community support is vital. Finding an Alopecia Support Squad (A$$) is imperative. Knowing there are others out there navigating the same storm and connecting with them provides a sense of solidarity for those who suffer. Whether online or in person, there are so many ways to find others who understand these struggles.

It is my ultimate goal that my clients walk away not just with knowledge about the options available for their hair, but also with a firm understanding that they have support on this journey. The fear of losing hair, especially due to chemotherapy, is a very real and valid concern, but it doesn't define their strength or their identity.

As Celeste left my office after her consultation, a small smile broke through her previously anxious demeanor. Armed with information and a solid plan, she felt empowered to tackle the path ahead. I could see it in her eyes—she was ready to take on cancer, hair loss and all. In those moments, I'm reminded of what this work truly means. It's not just about preserving hair; it's about preserving hope, identity, and the courage to rise above the challenges ahead.

Beyond Chemo – Types of Hair Loss

Many people don't know that chemotherapy is not the only cause of alopecia. By definition, the term alopecia simply means abnormal loss of hair. Alopecia affects millions.

There are different types of Alopecia, but the main types include:

Alopecia Areata (AA), or patchy alopecia: one, multiple, separate, or conjoined smooth patches on the scalp

Alopecia Totalis (AT): total hair loss on the scalp

Alopecia Universalis (AU): total hair loss in all areas of the body

Androgenic Alopecia (AGA): hair loss due to hormones or genetics (female or male pattern baldness)

Telogen Effluvium (TE): temporary hair loss due to stress, illness, hormonal changes, or other factors

Anagen Effluvium (AE): hair shedding due to chemotherapy, radiation, or certain medical conditions

Postpartum Hair Loss: temporary hair loss, (i.e. telogen effluvium) experienced after childbirth, due to hormonal changes or other factors

Central Centrifugal Cicatricial Alopecia (CCCA): a scarring hair loss characterized by inflammation and damage to hair follicles, resulting in permanent hair loss in the affected areas

Traction Alopecia (TA): hair loss from tension or pulling on the hair, from certain hairstyles such as tight ponytails, braids, or weaves

Trichotillomania (TTM): an uncontrollable urge to pull out one's own hair, leading to noticeable hair loss.

As trichologists, we serve as paramedical professionals and do not diagnose medical conditions. However, we specialize in hair and scalp maladies and can identify varying types of alopecia. Each form of alopecia has specific traits and characteristics that make it easier to classify.

No matter what the type of alopecia, it can cause people of all genders to feel shame, causing deep emotional and mental pain and the loss of many lives.

Just like the visibility of breast cancer awareness campaigns and the prevalence of support groups have helped make it easier for women to cope with this illness, we need equally recognizable alopecia awareness campaigns and to offer support for those losing their hair, too!

Practicing What I Preach

Following the birth of my children, I experienced postpartum hair loss. So, the feelings my clients experience are very familiar to me.

In addition, many people who live with alopecia are bullied, which is something I've also experienced. As a young girl, I was bullied, felt isolated, and was made to feel like I didn't fit in. What I now practice, teach, speak, and share with others globally, on various major platforms, stems not only from my years of hair expertise, but from years of emotional healing.

Healing doesn't happen instantaneously or overnight; it takes time. The journey can be daunting and uncertain, and I believe that no single event or person can define your self-esteem. However, if you can take one day at a time to practice building a positive self-image, you can make a difference in your life.

In assisting hundreds of women on their journeys with alopecia, and through my own journey, I realized that when we use an affirmation as a simple tool of encouragement, we can help people with alopecia embrace their individuality and we can help increase their self-esteem and self-confidence. We all crave acceptance and simply want to feel "okay" in our skin.

Proverbs 18:21 (NIV), states, "The tongue has the power of life and death, and those who love it will eat its fruit." Practice speaking love, life, and goodness over yourself with positive affirmations, quotes, songs, etc.

Whether you have hair loss, struggle with self-esteem, or appearance-related issues, or support those who do, I advise you to make it a priority to become your own best advocate.

Your body changes physiologically in reaction to the ideas that go through your mind each moment of every day. Your brain sends signals and releases neurotransmitters simply by thinking about something. Almost all of your body's processes, including your emotions and moods, are controlled by these chemicals.

Affirmations, also known as self-affirmations, are ideas you consciously think in order to strengthen, inspire, and relax your mind and body. They can be uplifting assertions that are used to contradict pessimistic, depressive, or anxiety-inducing ideas and attitudes. As you navigate alopecia and its emotional effects, you can use affirmations to change your moods, thought patterns, and behavioral routines.

Positive affirmations can be transformative.

By using affirmations, you can acknowledge your strengths and be gentle with your weaknesses. You can also be a source of support for others who may be struggling with their own self-image.

Self-esteem impacts how we think, act, and feel—not just about ourselves, but also in relation to others.

Our level of self-esteem profoundly influences how we navigate life and our ability to achieve our goals, whether that's overcoming social stigma or pursuing personal aspirations.

When we feel good about ourselves, we radiate happiness and attract positive relationships. Embracing self-love is the foundation of high self-esteem. It empowers us to face challenges, enrich our lives, and maintain both confidence and adaptability. It allows us to foster a "can do" attitude that instills pride in ourselves.

Creating a Movement

During that initial consultation with Celeste many years back, learning how psychologically unmanageable losing her hair was to her, I increased my resolve to help my clients not only navigate their outward appearance with cranial prostheses, but also to create tools to provide emotional support.

I created #alopeciaaffirmations to start a movement and challenge the social stigma. Here are five you can share on your favorite social media platform:

1. Your alopecia does not define you; your inner qualities shine through.
2. Your hair does not determine your self-worth.
3. Love and accept yourself, with hair or no hair at all, unconditionally.
4. You are deserving of love and respect, regardless of your appearance.
5. You are empowered to define your own standards of beauty.

I invite you to share these empowering affirmations for millions like Celeste, suffering from hair loss, and to craft personal ones using "I am" to manifest your best self. There's no limit to the positivity you can create.

As we all share affirmations for and with each other, we will build a community of support... and ultimately save lives.

Trichologist Stephanie Anderson, DPC, MPC, BSM is a global speaker and author. She has been featured on NBC, ABC, CBS, Fox News, and more. As an advocate for alopecia awareness, her mission is to educate and foster empathy and empowerment. To learn more, visit StephanieLAnderson. com and follow her @trinitylacewigs.

How to Protect People with Disabilities from Partnership Abuse

by Shāna Boutté

In 2017, I entered into what was meant to be a marriage but turned out to be nothing more than a ceremony that led to a life of hardship and abuse. For the first eight days, including the wedding night, there was no affection, passionate kissing, or touching, as I had imagined.

As a woman with more than 13 neurological and learning disabilities, including autism, dyslexia, and ADHD, I cannot read facial expressions often, incorrectly interpret body language, and miss many social cues. Picking up on the intentions and subtleties of others is not second nature to me. Unfortunately, I soon discovered that having these vulnerabilities would make me an easy target for partnership abuse, something that would become the context of this relationship throughout the next two years of my life.

During this time, I faced a debilitating illness that left me partially paralyzed from the waist down, and at one point, the doctors gave me just five weeks to live.

Being in graduate school, I was dependent on the man I had married for my survival in both the physical and academic realms. He even controlled my social media accounts and online activity and investments.

Instead of support, I received neglect. When I needed assistance getting to the bathroom, it was rarely given. When I really was thirsty and at risk for dehydration, he gave me one glass of water per day. Being unable to lift a pan or plate from the shelf made cooking impossible, as did not being able to stand to cook, so I received one meal a day.

Even with my Social Security disability, my medical expenses each month could not be met, so my parents helped. He took half my disability check each month. Eventually, all of my retirement savings and most of my jewelry vanished, even though it was in a safe. I did not have a camera on it, but he was the only person who knew I had it or where it was.

My parents couldn't cover all the necessary costs. The one who should have been my partner only added to my burden.

He held me at gunpoint more than 30 times. Each time, the gun was a foot or less from me, and each time, he threatened his own suicide, provoking horrifying images that haunted me all day in class or at my internship. These threats were more than just words—they were psychological torture, designed to keep me in a state of fear and under control.

The abuse extended beyond the physical and emotional realms. I was also being drained financially. Money was siphoned from me for years, and my credit cards were compromised repeatedly. This had occurred for more than five years when an international forensic analyst uncovered the extent of the harm and manipulation. We discovered that my email was not the primary email on all my linked social media accounts, which also linked to payment methods. I was being watched, and my online activity was being controlled without my knowledge.

He claimed that because Jesus died for our sins, there was no such thing as sin. Based on his explanation, my understanding is this gave him an excuse in his mind to justify any action to manipulate, control, and attack me spiritually.

Eventually, we divorced, but in order for him to leave, a hefty payoff was negotiated between him and my family. With my parents present, I heard him say, "I never loved you," and "You were just a place to stay," which disgustingly validated my feelings and summarized the treatment I received for two years. My self-worth and sense of belonging were dissolved, and the harm from him continued even after the divorce. He took much of my property when he left, including my medically necessary adaptive equipment, which was extending my life expectancy.

The week my divorce was finalized in 2020, I managed to complete graduate school with a 3.9 grade point average. Coming from a nonverbal background, I was denied access to graduate school for 14 consecutive years due to my autism, according to the dean of the psychology department.

With a history of special education from kindergarten through my senior year of high school, I was told I would never graduate from high school and never go to college. Throughout college, there were countless challenges and no support for disabled students like me.

I attribute this accomplishment entirely to walking with God and my faith in the Trinity. I believe it's a testament to the power of faith and the strength that comes from believing in, walking with, and witnessing that God is greater than any challenge.

My parents were my lifeline, the earthly representation of our Heavenly Father. Their love and support were crucial to my survival. Once I acknowledged the abuse, I began to reach out to a small circle of friends who helped me navigate the legal and personal challenges that followed.

I now live in a disability house where I face many daily challenges—neurological disabilities are lifelong. But meeting new people is easy again, and creating new friendships is joyful.

There is also the reality of him knowing where I live, so I've installed a home security system and changed all the locks. Safety is a priority in ways I could not have imagined before the wedding.

My faith grows daily, and it's what kept me alive during the healing period after graduation since legal separation does not guarantee safety. Therapy and spiritual coaching became essential for my recovery. I continue to see a therapist, and as a mental health professional who specializes in intellectual, developmental, and trauma disabilities, I had to step back from working with trauma cases while I healed.

As always, forgiveness became my personal goal—one that was both spiritual and emotional. It has always been within me to forgive others, and he is no exception. Forgiving him was the easy part of forgiveness, but because I introduced him to my family, whom he had harmed, the self-blame made living challenging. The hardest part of forgiveness was forgiving myself.

Once I did, my life changed, and blessings beyond what I could imagine began to flow. This is also when my nightmares began to subside, and the trauma I suffered could feel like it was in the past most of the time, rather than in the present as it did before I compassionately forgave myself.

Because of these events, and predominantly because of walking in fire with faith, I was blessed with an idea that I believe was given to me by God. I give Him all the credit for what this encompasses. Even in the darkest times, I found the will to survive and succeed, not because of any human support, but because of the Divine, the Beloved, in my life. What is seemingly impossible is attainable in the miracle realm. I manifest and live in miracles.

The idea was for a program called Partnership Protection. While still in its early phases of development, the goals of this non-government-supported program are:

1) To provide financial independence and possibly safe housing to survivors to prevent further abuse, reducing the risk of returning to violent environments. Companies would have established accounts set aside for escape, food, and other necessities as part of an alternate plan to aid victims in reaching safety, and these funds would be supported by those who pay into the accounts such as employers, employees, survivors, and victims.

2) To provide mentorship, guidance, and support for those facing partnership abuse. Mentors will encourage getting and staying out of the situation by sharing how *they* got

away from *their* abusers and assisting victims in areas of need. Survival stories mentors have may improve means of escape through shared knowledge and experience.

3) To educate and spread awareness on what constitutes partnership abuse—to help victims and those who would help empower victims to recognize the signs and the personal protection we can provide to ourselves as we journey away from harm. Isolation is a key tactic of abusers' control, and it makes a victim's network of support very small.

What I want others to learn from my experience is that abuse is not always visible to the person experiencing it. I didn't see abuse or control, and it took others to point it out. Without the intervention of my loving in-laws, who were the first people to recognize abuse and help me get out of the situation, who knows how much worse it could have become?

Some common examples of abuse include:

- Isolation
- Insults
- Misquoting scripture or sacred texts to confuse or manipulate
- Stealing or withholding money
- Comparing a partner's features, clothes, makeup, and style to others
- Cultural abuse (having one's culture used against them)
- Social class abuse (having one's socioeconomic status used against them)
- Identity-based abuse
- Exploitation
- Neglect
- Refusing to offer love or support when it is needed

- Forcing a person to engage in domestic labor
- Taking photos of an unkept living space when a person is too ill to clean and/or threatening to show others photos of a mess.

These forms of abuse often cause victims to question themselves rather than the abuser, leading to further entrapment.

Partnership Protection will be an empowerment program, both cross-cultural and cross-religious, offering suggestions for preventing and addressing abuse in different countries represented at the United Nations, where I spoke on this topic.

The program would include safety teams in workplaces and educational institutions that could help those in abusive situations by creating and providing essential survival resources.

The voice of the victim is essential in their healing process, and Partnership Protection would prioritize this, allowing survivors to take control of their recovery from abuse. Autonomy is so important to a person who is learning a new space in the world and discovering a sense of value they may have never experienced, so in this mindful-based transpersonal program, survivors would have a say in their healing modalities and the freedom to choose their support team based on their needs. This might include spiritual leaders, friends, family, and mental health providers. This is part of the process of becoming powerful instead of powerless. We learn to use our voice through this part of healing. And participants will want to know how to break the cycle they are in, not just receive basic needs like shelter and clothing.

Mentorship is crucial in breaking the cycle of abuse. Survivors who have successfully escaped abusive situations can share their stories and strategies with those still trapped. This shared knowledge can be a powerful tool in helping others find a way out. Additionally, offering survivors jobs in mentorship roles can help them remain financially independent, reducing the risk of falling into more abusive situations.

Survivors of abuse could work in the program, using their experiences to help others escape similar situations. This mentorship would provide not only practical support but also emotional and spiritual guidance, helping victims build a new life free from abuse by not depending on anyone else for financial security.

Partnership Protection would also offer support based on Maslow's Hierarchy of Needs and other humanist perspectives, ensuring that survivors receive comprehensive care.

Abusers who want to change also have access to care and support in Partnership Protection, because the atmosphere of person-centered care is free of judgment.

This mindful-based program can teach alternatives to quick reactions to dysregulated emotions with the assistance of executive function specialists, among other types of therapists and spiritual leaders.

Many people with disabilities are trapped in abusive relationships, with no way out. By creating programs like Partnership Protection, disabled women and other at-risk populations would have access to tools they need to escape, recover, and eventually, thrive. This is a road to independence and leaving trauma in the past through layers of healing. Partnership Protection is a community where no woman needs to heal alone or navigate trauma silently.

The journey to recovery from domestic partnership abuse is long and difficult, but with faith, support, and a commitment to change, we can help survivors rebuild their lives and find the strength to move forward.

By working together, we can ensure that no one is trapped or forced to endure what I went through, and that those who are currently suffering have a way out. Whether it's through developing new programs, offering support, or simply raising awareness, everyone has a role to play in ending partnership abuse.

Let us come together to protect the most vulnerable among us. Love is an action, a verb, and it's what we do. Together, we can create a world where everyone, regardless of their abilities, can live free from fear and abuse.

Award-winning public speaker, author, and licensed coach, Shāna Boutté, MA, IMC, MLC, is a mindful-based mental health expert with over 20 years of experience supporting individuals with disabilities. With more than 13 disabilities, including autism, she's a certified advocate for human rights and disability law. Learn more at shanaboutte.com.

Three Steps to Your PATH to Thrive

by Britt Ivy Boice

I was strapped into a cold metal gurney, staring at the ceiling of an ambulance in excruciating pain. I felt like I was lying on a bed of knives. Fifteen hours earlier, I'd been in complete denial of everything happening in my body, and most importantly, was determined not to go to the hospital. The last time I had gone to a hospital, my dad, my hero, had died.

Fifteen minutes before, my neighbor had called 911 after she'd found me passed out on the bedroom floor of my apartment. She'd heard my screams from across the apartment complex, and now, here I was, surrounded by EMTs who were fighting for my life.

The sound of the sirens from the ambulance they'd wheeled me into was deafening. But it took less than a minute for the IV they put in my arm to do its magic. I began to move from total agony to "la la land," or Heaven, or wherever it was.

As my vision blurred out, it occurred to me that I might be dying. I looked one of the paramedics right in the eye and asked, "Do you know Jesus?" As a strong believer, I figured if I was going to Heaven, I was taking someone with me!

At the ER ten minutes later, surrounded by the blaring beeps of the machines they were hooking me up to just to keep me alive, the doctor announced that in the past 24 hours, at just 39 years old, I'd had a massive, life-threatening heart attack.

As his words sank in, I directed my thoughts to God. "Are you serious?! Like I haven't been through enough in my life?!"

I thought of all the times I had considered suicide and not gone through with it. Even though I was surrounded by a cast of people trying to save my life, at that moment, I felt absolutely alone, afraid, and abandoned, even by the God I loved.

I had learned that when you don't eat properly, your heart will feed off the muscle for nourishment and begin to cannibalize itself, but before the heart attack, it didn't matter to me. I kept on with the disordered eating because I wanted to be "perfect."

This is one of many things that went wrong while I was suffering from this debilitating prison. An eating disorder affects your whole body. And it affects your whole life. Just like any addiction, it completely hijacks your priorities and comes before your responsibilities and commitments. My personal life and relationships were in shambles.

I decided I couldn't go through another heart attack again. I realized that trying to be thin and following unrealistic beauty standards sold in the media was killing me. It really hit home that I needed to either stop starving myself or end it all.

It all started at 17 years old when I left the safe nest of my parents' home in Palo Alto for the beautiful world of Santa Barbara, California. Out of the many options I had, I picked my undergraduate

S.T.O.R.Y. Compiled by Dr. Elayna Fernández

university because it looked like it came right out of a Hollywood beach movie set. Yet, navigating college turned out to be more challenging than I'd anticipated. I ended up making choices that would irrevocably alter the course of my life.

Even though I wasn't raised to party, I ended up drinking and drugging to fit in with college friends.

Even though I hated smoking, I smoked to fit in. Lung cancer and death didn't scare me, but not fitting into society's standards did. I wanted to fit in so badly, I was willing to die.

Even though I was voted nanny of the year in my hometown and loved kids, I said yes to ending pregnancies.

Terrified, alone, and scared to tell my parents, I shared my situation with a new girlfriend at school who seemed to fit in. She had boyfriends, was invited to parties, and always looked put together, with a movie star hairstyle and artistically done makeup. She matter-of-factly informed me, "I had an abortion and know exactly where to take you to handle the problem."

I was told that abortion had no side effects and that everything would be "just fine."

I fell for that lie hook, line, and sinker.

Over the next few years, I cycled in and out of depression, self-sabotage, addiction, suicidal thinking, eating disorders, and unhealthy relationships. I went to great lengths to keep the look good going, yet in reality, I was living in pain, haunted by a mystery I couldn't solve.

Fast forward to several years after the abortions, when a God-ordained "coincidence" helped me understand why I struggled for so many years.

I was on my way home to Oregon from Seattle, Washington, when I heard the airport loudspeaker blaring:

"Passenger Ivy, passenger Britt Ivy! Last call, gate 24!"

I bolted out of the coffee shop line and flew down the moving escalator to Gate 24, flashed my ticket to the uniformed agent, and boarded a packed plane. Because of many delays and plane changes due to weather, there was no assigned seating. There were row after row of men in business suits, and I was thinking, "There must be a convention somewhere!"

I spotted one empty seat and asked the woman sitting at the window seat, "May I sit here?"

She looked like an older Florence Henderson, the mom from *The Brady Bunch*, with her pixie haircut and kind eyes. She gave me a strange look and said, "Uh, sure."

When you don't want someone to sit next to you on an airplane, you pile your stuff there, and that's what she had done. Exasperated from having to move her purse, her book, and her coat, she blurted out, "I'm just trying to get home to my husband in Oregon. After all these weather delays, now I'm waiting for some "Passenger Ivy!"

I wanted to disappear.

I plopped into the seat. Mrs. Brady Bunch introduced herself as Ginny and told me she had just visited her granddaughter, who

S.T.O.R.Y. Compiled by Dr. Elayna Fernández

was attending college in Seattle. She asked which college I had attended. Normally, I'm mute when I fly. Instead, I started a monologue about my college years, my mistakes, and my poor decisions, telling her about my desire to fit in with the popular crowd.

When I looked up from my monologue and connected eyes with Ginny, the tears I'd been holding back for years busted out like the Hoover Dam. There I was, black mascara streaking down my face in front of a complete stranger, bawling.

At first, she politely looked away as I cried, but after a minute or two of this, she touched my hand and asked, "Would you like a tissue?"

For the next two hours, this woman who had never laid eyes on me before handed me tissue after tissue, while I poured my guts out about my college sweetheart and the joys and the sorrows we went through.

When we were about to land, Ginny reached into her purse, handed me a pamphlet, and said, "Take a look at this."

I grasped the pamphlet and read, "Do you suffer from self-sabotage, eating disorders, addiction, abusive relationships, suicidal thinking?"

I turned to her and exclaimed, "They know me!"

She said, "Why don't you turn that pamphlet over?"

When I did, I saw three words that changed my life. Suddenly, my life made sense. The penny dropped. It read "P.A.T. - Post Abortion Trauma."

131

It turned out that all the self-sabotage, eating disorders, abusive relationships, addictions, and other unconscious self-destructive behavior was post-traumatic stress from the abortions. All the drama and trauma I'd been living with and beating myself up for was screaming to be addressed. PTSD from abortion is subtle, yet devastating to living a successful life.

The plane landed. Ginny and I shared a long hug and exchanged phone numbers.

Over the next year, I had time to pray and reflect, and, similar to after the heart attack, I realized my choices were killing me. I found myself unsatisfied and unable to achieve the peace I wanted to enjoy in all areas of my life. I longed to find a path to thrive.

At first, it felt like a struggle to step into the person God had always intended for me to be. It wasn't a magical transformation overnight.

It took time, patience, and a willingness to surrender my will to God. But slowly, I began to feel different. I felt lighter, more whole, and less burdened by the weight of my past mistakes and regrets.

The chains that had held me captive for so long were loosening. I wasn't the same person I had been before the heart attack, before the years of self-sabotage, and before I met Ginny. I had changed, and for the first time in years, I was beginning to feel hope again.

There were days when it felt like I was walking through a fog, unsure of which direction to take. But I learned that walking by faith didn't always mean having all the answers. Sometimes, it meant taking one small step at a time, trusting that God would lead me where I needed to go. My life wasn't perfect—far from it—but I could see that with each step of faith, I was moving closer to wholeness.

The healing process was not just about getting better emotionally and spiritually; it also meant taking care of my body. I had neglected my health for so long, punishing myself for my failures and starving my body to fit into a mold I thought was ideal. But God was teaching me that my body was a temple, and it deserved love and respect. I began to eat better, exercise, and sleep. I learned to listen to my body instead of ignoring its cries for help. I also started to set boundaries in my relationships. I had spent years in toxic friendships and romantic relationships, always trying to please others and ignore my own needs. But now, I understood the importance of surrounding myself with people who truly loved and supported me, people who encouraged me to grow and thrive. I wasn't afraid to let go of relationships that were draining me and pulling me back into old habits. Instead, I invested in people who inspired me, who uplifted me, and who pointed me toward the Lord.

My journey wasn't always easy. There were setbacks, challenges, and moments of doubt. But I learned to lean into the process, knowing that healing wasn't always linear. There were days when I wanted to give up, when the pain of my past seemed too much to bear. But I pressed on.

Through this process, I found my voice. For so long, I had been silent, ashamed of the choices I had made and the pain I had caused. But now, I was ready to speak. I wanted to share my story, to help others who were stuck in the same patterns of self-doubt, shame, and brokenness. I realized that my pain, my scars, and my struggles weren't something to hide but something that could be used to help others. It wasn't easy to open up and be vulnerable, but I knew that God had given me a platform to speak from, and I wanted to use it for His glory.

I chose to lean into my faith, select a mentor, and surround myself with a loving community and family. I began to be who God made me to be. I like to call it Britt 2.0. The more authentic me. The better me.

That's when I started to speak on stages to share my message. I was overwhelmed by the response. Women from all over the world reached out to me, telling me how my story had touched their hearts. Some of them had experienced the same kind of trauma and loss that I had. Some were struggling with eating disorders, addiction, or abusive relationships. Others were facing the aftermath of abortion and didn't know where to turn. But they all had one thing in common—they were looking for hope. And I realized that by sharing my journey, I was giving them just that.

As I continued to speak and share my message, I began to see a common thread among the women I encountered. So many of them were walking through life with unhealed wounds, holding onto the pain of their past, afraid to move forward. They were stuck in cycles of self-doubt and shame, believing that they weren't worthy of healing or happiness. But I knew better. I had lived it. And I was living proof that transformation was possible.

That's when I decided to become a coach. I wanted to empower women to break free from the chains of their past and step into the life God had called them to live. I wanted to help them discover their worth, their purpose, and their power. Through coaching, I was able to walk alongside women, guiding them through the process of healing and growth, just as I had healed with the help of my mentor, Ginny.

Steadily, I began to see the fruit of my labor. Women were healing. They were thriving. They were becoming their 2.0 selves.

Now, through the grace of God, I'm a bestselling author and speaker, and I continue to empower women to become their 2.0 selves. My personal transformation led me to share the tools which successfully guided me through not just healing from abortion, but moving forward. Today, I'm most fulfilled empowering Christ-centered women to overcome their trauma and thrive.

I am no longer defined by my past. I am no longer a slave to my mistakes or my pain. I am a daughter of the King, and I know that my best days are ahead of me. I am thriving, not just surviving. And I believe that you can, too. You can step into your own 2.0 self. You can heal. You can thrive. And with God by your side, you can do anything.

So, if you're reading this today and you're feeling stuck, broken, or lost, I want you to know that you are not alone. You are not defined by your mistakes. You are not defined by your past. You are loved, you are worthy, and you are capable of great things. The same God who healed me can heal you. The same God who redeemed my life can redeem yours. And together, we can walk the path to healing and transformation.

If you have wasted time and energy and find yourself on the wrong path like the millions of women who are walking around the world not knowing why their life isn't working, you can heal for real with The One who holds babies in Heaven. You are loved.

Taking some simple steps can help free you from a life of self-sabotage and take you where you dream to go.

Become your 2.0 self using the acronym PATH:

P - Pray or Ponder. Ask whatever higher power you believe in to provide guidance to become your best self.

"Rejoice always, pray without ceasing, in everything give thanks; for this is the will of God in Christ Jesus for you." 1 Thessalonians 5:16-18

A - Accept and Assess your current state. Take some time with yourself to frankly assess your current state of health, physical, mental, financial, and spiritual. Reflect on ways to uplevel your life.

"Beloved, I wish above all things that you prosper and be in health, even as your soul prospers." 3 John 1:2

T - Trust. Trust in the process is a universal truth. Healing, growth, and progress take time. It's about trusting that your efforts today will pay off in the long run. Trust that you have what it takes, even if you don't have all the answers right now. Trust there are no coincidences that you are reading this chapter, and acknowledge you're right where you need to be.

"Trust in the Lord with all your heart, And lean not on your own understanding; In all your ways acknowledge Him, And He shall direct your paths." Proverbs 3:5-6

H - Hope. Hope is an essential step on your path to thrive. It's what keeps you moving forward when things feel heavy or uncertain. Cultivating hope involves setting small, achievable goals and celebrating the little wins along the way. Having a clear vision of where you want to go and taking consistent action toward it is an essential part of keeping hope alive.

"For I know the plans I have for you, declares the Lord, plans for welfare and not for evil, to give you a future and a hope." Jeremiah 29:11

As I look back on everything that led me to this point, I can't help but be in awe of God's faithfulness. He took a broken, lost woman, someone who had been on the brink of death, and He redeemed her. He used my pain, my mistakes, and my trauma to bring about a greater purpose. And He is still using me to help others find the healing and hope that only He can provide.

Today, Ginny has been my best friend and mentor for 22 years. I believe that "coincidence" is when God chooses to remain anonymous. Like the "coincidence" that I sat next to Ginny. Or the "coincidence" that she happened to be the Board of Directors President for a Pregnancy Care and Adoption Center.

One summer, Ginny and I were speaking at a women's retreat. She and I were on stage at the podium, and in front of the whole audience, she turned to me and said, "Britt, I never did understand why you had to sit next to me on that plane?"

I gave her a strange look. "Ginny, I had to sit next to you. That was the only seat open!" She turned to me slowly and said, "Britt, that plane was almost empty."

We stared at each other in silence as we comprehended the enormity of the miracle. To this day, we believe that plane was filled with angels so I'd have to sit next to Ginny, and I'd have to change my life.

There's no fulfillment in just surviving. Step out of fear and into the faith of knowing you were created brilliantly to THRIVE! You are beautiful just the way you are. I completely believe God has more in store for you, and I want to help you get there.

Remember, you are a masterpiece in progress. You are a woman of strength, purpose, and beauty. And with God's help, you will become the 2.0 version of yourself—stronger, braver, and more beautiful than ever before. Keep going. You've got this.

Founder of Heartlife Foundation, Britt Ivy, "The Courage Coach," is an award-winning television host, bestselling author, philanthropist, and speaker. Britt empowers women who have ended a pregnancy to bravely live with hope and purpose through her program, PATH2Thrive. Learn more at BrittIvy.com/Path-2-Thrive

Your Power to Thrive

by Dr. Elayna Fernández

I am proud of you for investing time in reading these stories and for considering the ideas and solutions each author offered in this book.

You, too, can become a Transformational Storyteller.

The root word of transform is the Latin word *transformare*, which is a combination of the prefix trans- and the word *formare*:

- Trans-*: A prefix that means "across"
- Formare: A word that means "to form"

The word transform means to change something from one form, appearance, structure, or type to another. It is not about fixing or helping, but seeing our potential and serving each other as we move across to the form—or identity—that was meant for us. This is why we think of a caterpillar turning into a butterfly.

Writing your transformational S.T.O.R.Y. will reveal the transformation you've already experienced. It will allow you to see the butterfly essence that is already within you, while embracing the growth that is necessary in your caterpillar parts.

Telling your transformational S.T.O.R.Y. will inspire others to transform as you have. They will learn from your wisdom and take action that will lead them to thrive.

As I always say, "When you feel unworthy, unloved, or unwell, read a story. Tell your story." Use your story as your therapeutic elixir to your present, your link to the past, and your ticket to impact the future.

Through storytelling, we can spread ideas that will heal the world and enable us to thrive together.

Blessings,

Edlayna

References

Chapter 1 - Carmen Paredes:

McKinsey & Company. "Women in the Workplace 2023." McKinsey & Company, 2023, https://www.mckinsey.com/featured-insights/diversity-and-inclusion/women-in-the-workplace.

Catalyst. "Why Diversity and Inclusion Matter: Quick Take." Catalyst, 23 June 2020, https://www.catalyst.org/research/why-diversity-and-inclusion-matter/.

McKinsey & Company. "Women in the Workplace 2021." McKinsey & Company, 2021, https://www.mckinsey.com/featured-insights/diversity-and-inclusion/women-in-the-workplace.

Bersin, Josh, et al. "High-Impact Diversity and Inclusion: Maturity Model and Top Findings."

Deloitte Insights, 2021, https://www2.deloitte.com/us/en/insights/focus/human-capital-trends/2021/diversity-and-inclusion-maturity-model.html.

Great Place to Work. "Data Shows Inclusive Cultures Deliver 27% Higher Profitability." Great Place to Work, 2022, https://www.greatplacetowork.com/resources/blog/data-shows-inclusive-cultures-deliver-27-higher-profitability.

Tsedal Neeley and Paul Leonardi. "How Inclusive Leaders Make Their Teams Feel Heard." Harvard Business Review, 22 Mar. 2022, https://hbr.org/2022/03/how-inclusive-leaders-make-their-teams-feel-heard.

Chapter 2 - Dr. Zoe-Ann Bartlett:

Global Peace Index (GPI) from Institute for Economics & Peace (IEP) June 2024

University of Cambridge; Centre for the Future of Democracy. A World Divided Oct 2022

Pew Research Center; Trend Magazine; Global Migration's Rapid Rise; Summer 2016

United Nations; Climate Change, Current: WHO; Climate Change, Oct 2023

Causes and Consequences of Income Inequality: A Global Perspective; IMF June 2015

WHO, WHO Commission on Social Connection; Nov 2023

Chapter 3 - Lidia Molinara:

World Health Organization (2023). Patient safety. https://www.who.int/news-room/fact-sheets/detail/patient-safety

Chapter 4 - Dr. Elayna Fernández:

A. Dealy, "Using Evaluation Data To Motivate and Persuade," presentation at the Garrett Lee Smith Campus Grantee Meeting, Orlando, Florida, February 4, 2010.

Institute for Health Metrics and Evaluation (IHME). Global Burden of Disease Study 2021 (GBD 2021): Deaths and DALYs. Seattle, WA, 2024.

Cerel, Julie, et al. "How Many People Are Affected by Suicide?" Psychiatric Services, vol. 69, no. 1, 2018, pp. 32-37. DOI: 10.1176/appi.ps.201700235.

"Best Practices and Recommendations for Reporting on Suicide." Reporting on Suicide, 2024, www.reportingonsuicide.org.

Maté, Gabor. When the Body Says No: Exploring the Stress-Disease Connection. Wiley, 2003.

Google Books, https://books.google.com.do/books?id=3Y2t1oQEmcoC&printsec =frontcover&source=gbs_ge_summary_r&redir_esc=y#v=onepage&q&f =false.

Fava, Giovanni A., et al. "Definition of Treatment-Resistant Depression: A Meta-Analysis." Psychiatric Clinics of North America, vol. 40, no. 2, 2017, pp. 247-267.

PubMed Central, https://pmc.ncbi.nlm.nih.gov/articles/PMC5341764/.

Levine, Peter A., and Gabor Maté. "The Wisdom of Trauma: Gabor Maté and Peter Levine in Conversation About How the Body Heals from Trauma." Pace Connection, 2021, https://www.pacesconnection.com/g/california-aces-action/blog/the-wisdom-of-trauma-gabor-mate-peter-levine-in-conversation-about-how-the-body-heals-from-trauma.

S.T.O.R.Y. Compiled by Dr. Elayna Fernández

Chapter 5 - Mirella Acebo:

Church Initiative. Grief Share: Your Journey from Mourning to Joy. Church Initiative, 1999

Abedi, Sarah. "Motherhood's Hidden Journey: Impact on Maternal Health." *Psychology Today*, 17 July 2024, www.psychologytoday.com/us/blog/healing-the-wounded-healers/202407/motherhoods-hidden-journey-impact-on-maternal-health.

Chapter 6 - Dr. Julie Radlauer:

Office of the Surgeon General (OSG). Our Epidemic of Loneliness and Isolation: The U.S. Surgeon General's Advisory on the Healing Effects of Social Connection and Community [Internet]. Washington (DC): US Department of Health and Human Services; 2023. Available from: https://www.ncbi.nlm.nih.gov/books/NBK595227/

Dewa, Lindsay H. et al. "Quality Social Connection as an Active Ingredient in Digital Interventions for Young People With Depression and Anxiety: Systematic Scoping Review and Meta-analysis." Journal of medical Internet research vol. 23,12 e26584. 17 Dec. 2021, doi:10.2196/26584

Pagan, Ricardo. "Gender and Age Differences in Loneliness: Evidence for People without and with Disabilities." International journal of environmental research and public health vol. 17,24 9176. 8 Dec. 2020, doi:10.3390/ijerph17249176

Othering & Belonging. Haas Institute for a Fair and Inclusive Society at the University of California, Berkeley, 2016.

Brown, Brené. Atlas of the Heart: Mapping Meaningful Connection and the Language of Human Experience. First edition. New York, Random House, 2021.

Granovetter, Mark S. "The Strength of Weak Ties." American Journal of Sociology, vol. 78, no. 6, 1973, pp. 1360–80. JSTOR, http://www.jstor.org/stable/2776392. Accessed 15 Nov. 2024.

Bruni, Luigino & Gilli, Mario & Pelligra, Vittorio. (2008). Reciprocity: theory and facts: Introduction to the special issue. International Review of Economics. 55. 10.1007/s12232-008-0042-9.

FEMpower: Transformational Stories of Women Thriving Against All Odds

Chapter 7 - Dr. Jiyoung Jung:

Cejalvo, Elena, et al. "Caregiving Role and Psychosocial and Individual Factors: A Systematic Review." Healthcare, vol. 9, no. 12, Dec. 2021, p. 1690. doi:10.3390/healthcare9121690.

Barnett, Whitney, et al. "Caregiver-child Proximity as a Dimension of Early Experience." Development and Psychopathology, vol. 34, 2022, pp. 647-665.

Jongedijk, Ruud A. "Narrative Exposure Therapy: An Evidence-Based Treatment for Multiple and Complex Trauma." European Journal of Psychotraumatology, vol. 5, Dec. 2014, p. 26522. doi:10.3402/ejpt.v5.26522.

Chapter 8 - Mary Ottman:

Ruehl, Emma. "Attrition: Definition, Types, Causes & Mitigation Tips." SHRM, 15 Apr. 2024, https://www.shrm.org/topics-tools/news/employee-relations/attrition-definition-types-causes-mitigation-tips#:~:text=The%20average%20annual%20turnover%20rate,%3A%20Human%20Capital%20Report%2C%202022. Accessed 4 Dec. 2024.

Casic, Ana. Pavlou, Christina. Gavala, Glota. Rader, Mark. Runft, April. Latta, Shannon. "What employees want from L&D in 2024." Talent LMS, https://www.talentlms.com/research/learning-development-trends. Accessed 4 Dec. 2024.

"4 in 10 Companies Will Replace Workers With AI in 2025." Resume Templates, 13 Aug. 2024, https://www.resumetemplates.com/4-in-10-companies-will-replace-workers-with-ai-in-2025/. Accessed 4 Dec. 2024.

Whiting, Geoff. "Understanding Employee Turnover Statistics and Trends for 2024." Hubstaff, 13 Aug. 2024, https://hubstaff.com/blog/employee-turnover-statistics/. Accessed 4 Dec 2024.

Chapter 9 - Amb. Dr. Catherine Utsalo:

National Institute of Health (NIH). "Uterine Fibroids: A Detailed Overview." National Institute of Health, 2023.

American Psychological Association (APA). "Grief and Loss: Emotional Impacts of Miscarriage." American Psychological Association, 2023.

Tutu, Desmond, and Mpho Tutu. The Book of Forgiving: The Fourfold Path for Healing Ourselves and Our World. HarperOne, 2014.

The Bible. Key scriptures (e.g., Isaiah 41:10, Matthew 11:28–30).

Harvard T.H. Chan School of Public Health. "The Impact of Nutrition on Women's Health." 2024.

UN Women. "Ending Stigma: Reproductive Health Advocacy." UN Women, 2024.

Brown, Brené. Rising Strong: The Reckoning. The Rumble. The Revolution. Spiegel & Grau, 2015.

Weil, Andrew. Spontaneous Healing: How to Discover and Enhance Your Body's Natural Ability to Maintain and Heal Itself. Knopf, 1995.

Obama, Michelle. Becoming. Crown Publishing, 2018.

Chapter 10 - Stephanie Anderson:

Rebora, A., & Guarrera, M. (2021). Why Do Not All Chemotherapy Patients Lose Their Hair? Answering an Intriguing Question. Skin appendage disorders, 7(4), 280–285.

Chapter 11 - Shāna Boutté:

McLeod, PhD., Saul. "Maslow's Hierarchy of Needs." Www.simplypsychology. com, 24 Jan. 2024, www.simplypsychology.com. Accessed 15 June, 2024.

Chapter 12 - Britt Ivy Boice:

Biggs, M. Antonia, et al. "Does Abortion Increase Women's Risk for Post-Traumatic Stress? Findings from a Prospective Longitudinal Cohort Study." *BMJ Open*, vol. 6, no. 2, BMJ, Jan. 2016, p. e009698, https://doi.org/10.1136/bmjopen-2015-009698.

López-Gil, José Francisco, et al. "Global Proportion of Disordered Eating in Children and Adolescents." *JAMA Pediatrics*, vol. 177, no. 4, American Medical Association, Feb. 2023, pp. 363–63, https://doi.org/10.1001/jamapediatrics.2022.5848.